# SETTING
# THE CHURCH
# of ENGLAND
*free*

'I think of the Church of England as finished, dead.
I think it will be disestablished and probably join forces with
the Free Churches and the Methodists.'

*Terry Waite, reported in* The Times, *12 December 2001*

' "Lord", Martha said to Jesus, "if you had been here,
my brother would not have died."
Jesus said to her, "Your brother will rise again...
I am the resurrection and the life... Do you believe this?"
"Yes, Lord," she told him, "I believe..." ' '

*John 11:21, 23, 25-27 NIV*

# SETTING
# THE CHURCH
# of ENGLAND
## *free*

EDITOR: MARK MILLS-POWELL

FOREWORD BY STEVEN CROFT

John Hunt
Publishing Limited

Copyright © 2003 John Hunt Publishing Ltd
46A West Street, Alresford, Hants SO24 9AU, U.K.
Tel: +44 (0) 1962 736880  Fax: +44 (0) 1962 736881
E-mail: office@johnhunt-publishing.com
www.johnhunt-publishing.com

Text: © 2003 The Contributors
Design: Andrew Milne Design

ISBN 1 849298 111 0

A CIP catalogue record for this book is available
from the British Library.

Printed in the UK by Ashford Colour Press

# Contents

## Sharing good practice

## A challenge

## PART III THE LEADERSHIP REQUIRED

### Responses

# Foreword

## STEVEN CROFT

The story of God's people down the ages demonstrates that both Israel and the Church have often been called to face moments of change. Such times of transition may be shaped by economic, social and cultural factors beyond the control of the people of God. Or else the Church itself may have contributed to the change: both through its own mistakes and through internal movements of renewal.

As we stand at the beginning of a new century, the Church of England finds itself facing a particular vocation to change, develop and respond to internal movements urging renewal, to a present shaped in part by its past mistakes and to significant developments in our wider society, both national and global.

There are always at least three temptations when facing such moments of opportunity and decision. The first is to despair and gloom. The changes themselves and the prospect of change overwhelm us. The signs of disaster are all around us. The end is nigh. The consequence for the Church is discouragement.

The second temptation is to denial and retreat. 'What change?' we cry. 'Twas ever thus. Ministers today have an easy time of it compared to when we were young.' As long as we remain with the particular set of priorities that we favour, everything will come right in the end. So we simply screen out the evidence that is inconvenient to us and continue as we were. The consequence for the Church is seeping irrelevance.

Yet the third, and in some ways opposite temptation, is to fall prey to facile analysis and instant solutions. In a desire to be comfortable we seek to depict what is happening around us in a few broad brush strokes, and prescribe 'straightforward' action in this or that direction. The consequence for the Church is wasted energy and disappointed hopes.

In Scripture and tradition, the discipline of discerning the times and seeing the way forward is rarely easy, and never without cost. It is the discipline and vocation of the prophet. It is a discipline that requires all the tools of vision: including the gathering of data, analysis and a testing of what is being said, as well as dialogue and prayerful discernment. We will need both the resources gathered by previous generations, and the insights of the worldwide Church.

It is this task of discernment and vision that is the springboard for this book of essays and responses. A variety of authors from different parts of the Church of England have contributed their perspectives. The hope is that what is presented here will provide resources and lines of enquiry for all of those engaged in discerning what the Spirit is saying to the Church. The result is neither despair, denial nor simple solutions, but a realistic and wise appraisal of the present situation combined with genuine hope and practical resources for the future.

*Steven Croft, Warden, Cranmer Hall, Durham.*

# Introduction

## MARK MILLS-POWELL

He shot into my vitals the arrows of his quiver;
I have become the laughing-stock of all my people,
the object of their taunt-songs all day long . . .
My soul is bereft of peace; I have forgotten what happiness is;
so I say, 'Gone is my glory, and all that I had hoped for from the LORD.'

The thought of my affliction and my homelessness
is wormwood and gall . . .
But this I call to mind, and therefore I have hope:
The steadfast love of the LORD never ceases,
his mercies never come to an end;
they are new every morning; great is your faithfulness.
'The LORD is my portion,' says my soul, 'therefore I will hope in him.'

*Lamentations 3:13-24 NRSV*

When I mentioned to a friend in a Benedictine community that I was working on a book addressing the Church of England's future, he said, 'That will be a short book.' I didn't laugh, which was perhaps ungracious. While I knew what he was communicating through his joke, I was both more confident and too intense about the urgency of the situation to relax into laughter.

Another friend, after reading a number of the initial chapters, suggested, 'Mark, please find a way to avoid each essay beginning by saying that the Church of England is in a mess.' I have not done the radical editing she advocated for two reasons: first, I've wanted each of these voices to tell their own story; secondly, though it is true a number of contributions begin in that way (a number do not), it is time to be honest. A long time ago, Jürgen Moltmann taught me through his writings that every crisis is an opportunity. The desert is not only the place of pilgrimage, but also of new life. One reader wrote that one or two of the pieces made him feel depressed. Why not? Jeremiah wept.

> Michael Riddell, a theologian based in New Zealand, writes:
>> The Christian Church is dying in the West. This painful fact is the cause of a great deal of avoidance by the Christian community... The terminally sick patient is somewhere between denial and bargaining... But as pastoral carers and theologians know, it is not a healthy state to remain in. W. Bruegemann has helped us to see that the starting point of moving on with God is a deep and heartfelt grief.[1]

One of the great joys of working on this book has been discovering like-minded folk. One of these has been Trevor Beeson (Dean Emeritus of Winchester Cathedral). It was only recently that I picked up his book, *The Bishops*. The relief finding someone of his seniority who could be so frank and open was enormous. In his analysis, he writes, 'All of today's bishops fall into the single category of pastoral-manager, with the strongest emphasis on manager.'[2]

Undoubtedly one of the catalysts in this book's inception was my experience of pastoral reorganisation. Beeson writes about the all too familiar dynamic:

> [This] raises the issue of the deployment of the Church's clerical resources, nearly all of which are engaged in parish work in residential communities. This cannot continue if a pioneering church is to carry out its mission by serving and influencing wider fields of human endeavour. It is also the case that the present parish-based ministry is in most places a long way from dynamic or even satisfactory. The uniting of several rural parishes under one, itinerant, rector has – in spite of all that is said and done about lay leadership – caused only a weakening of church life in all of them. In towns and cities the haphazard deployment of the clergy often reflects only a makeshift strategy and creates frustration, stress and exhaustion.
>
> *Trevor Beeson*[3]

I am simple enough to believe that the principles we see in operation in the Acts of the Apostles still work. I think that the chapters in this book by David and Janie Beales, Hugh Ellis, John Summers and others all bear witness to that. We may be in something of a mess as an institution, but God's creativity has not worn out. Thankfully, the alternatives to the tired old patterns are beginning to be articulated afresh for this generation and this hour. The writing and thinking of Steven Croft[4] and Ian Bradley,[5] for example, I find enormously hopeful. My hope is that this book will help to stimulate a much larger conversation about where we are now as a Church, and where we could be under God in ten years' time. God's arm is not shortened. Do we have ears to hear, and hearts and wills eager to obey, and make the necessary sacrifices?

The new Archbishop of Canterbury could be a powerful influence to accelerate an open process of discernment about our direction as a Church without the fear that perpetrators of 'outside the box' ideas might be punished. Much, almost too much, has already been written about Rowan Williams. But one of my greatest sources of confidence in the prospect of his primacy derives from the fact that he understands the monastic tradition. Is it ridiculous of me to dream that in fifty or a hundred years the British Isles could be described as a land of hermits or semi-eremetic (scattered praying) communities (as Egypt was by AD 400) rather than a land of parishes?

One of the most blessed providences of my life was that at the tender age of eighteen (straight from Eton) I fell into the heart of the Community of Celebration. The Community had grown out of the Episcopal Church of the Redeemer in Houston, Texas, where charismatic renewal had begun to take root in the 1960s. As a young adult, Graham Pulkingham (its leader and formerly Rector of the Church of the Redeemer) became for me a father-figure. The next five years were formative for me; yes, crazy sometimes, but inspiring for me and many others, and still now almost thirty years later. Those were exciting, heady days, and the vision lives on, ready to be transmuted, to take flesh again in a different form at a later time. The Holy Spirit is remarkably consistent, but his/her creative work is always particular to each individual situation and epoch.

The shorthand code I use to describe the continuing vision is apostolic and contemplative Christian community. This is what Hugh Ellis, in his chapter, calls a 'prayer-centred and mission-focused' relational way of being church. I see it functioning wherever and whenever the Christian Church has begun to make significant headway, whether it be in Egypt in the fourth century or in Moravian communities in Germany in the eighteenth century. The most personal symbol for me of this pattern probably focuses on Little Gidding, perhaps because of its quintessential Englishness. It does not matter to me whether the dominant prayer form is quiet or more explosive. The Wesley brothers certainly understood the complementarity of catholic and evangelical devotional practice. But there will be absolutely no spiritual life to share beyond the boundary of the Christian community, if the prayerfulness is not sufficiently sustained and intentional.

There are many people in addition to Graham Pulkingham and the Community of Celebration to whom I owe a very big debt of gratitude. First, I must express my thanks to all the contributors to this volume, some of whom I know have 'sweated blood' over their chapters. Next I want to thank all those who read drafts of the first contributions. If I have forgotten any, please forgive me: in no particular order, Anna Newton, Ann Morisy, Mike Hill, Eric James, Ken Leech, Patrick Phelan OSB, Patrick Sookhdeo.

Phil Tomson must be given the credit for writing all the introductory questions to each chapter. He worked extremely hard in a short space of time.

I am very grateful to the prayerful and concentrated space provided by the Community of the Servants of the Will of God (Crawley Down) where I did almost all of the focused work on this project, and to the unstinting hospitality of Elmore Abbey (Newbury, Berks). Almost each week for nearly eight years Elmore Abbey has been crucial in providing regular space for reflection and prayer.

To those with whom I've shared life closely in the Guild of St John the Divine and St Mary Magdalene and in the Benefice of Basildon with Aldworth and Ashampstead, I will always be indebted. My family, Dana (my wife), three daughters (Bridget, Phoebe and Rachel) and parents (Ros and Neil Mills) have been long-suffering and supportive as they've seen me in labour pains at times because of the issues touched on in this book.

Without my incredibly patient and wonderfully loyal secretary, Ann Cornford, this project would never have been completed and hardly begun. Lastly, I must thank my uncle and godfather, Preb. J. T. C. B. Collins for his amazing example of the sanctified life and for his unswerving commitment to the institution that calls itself the Church of England.

*Mark Mills-Powell, Linton near Cambridge*

**Notes**

[1] Michael Riddell, *Threshold of the Future*: Reforming the Church in the Post-Christian West; SPCK. 1998; W. Bruegemann, The Prophetic Imagination, Fortress Press, Philadelphia, 1978.

[2] Trevor Beeson, *The Bishops*, SCM, 2002, p.1.

[3] Trevor Beeson, op. cit., p. 232.

[4] Steven Croft, *Ministry in Three Dimensions*, DLT, 1999, and *Transforming Communities*, DLT, 2002.

[5] Ian Bradley, *Colonies of Heaven: Celtic Models for Today's Church*, DLT, 2000, and *Columba, Pilgrim and Penitent*, Wild Goose Publications, 1996.

## PART ONE

# THE SITUATION WE FACE

### THE FACT OF GOD

He who comes knocking on my door,
he who would see me crushed on the floor.
Can I believe – he raises me up,
or is my belief still at the rim of the cup,
doubting and tasting but fearing to sup?


I know he is there but where?
In stillness and silence what do I hear?
I am and I am said my God
And in truth I must strive and certainly nod
for I know as a fact – there is my God.

*Anna Newton*

# I. Nearing The Edge

## GEORGE LINGS

How can we work towards true and lasting change in the Church without compromising the integrity of its calling?

In looking at the ways in which positive change may be brought about, how do we live with church structures without eventually reverting to a default position in order to survive?

*George Lings is the Director of the Church Army's Research Unit, the Sheffield Centre. In 1993 he was awarded a Lambeth degree for his research into new expressions of church. He publishes a quarterly booklet called,* Encounters on the Edge.

*In this opening chapter he looks at churches on the edge.*

### A CRISIS?

In June 2002 The Times carried a suspicious reaction to the signing of the covenant towards unity by Church leaders. The author of the article clearly misunderstood the renewing and energising forces within the Churches, seeing them as lunatic fundamentalist but growing fringes. The event was dismissed as the huddling together of an endangered species. The article ended, '. . . it was not cynicism . . . when the ArchBish and his chums signed their covenant last week. It was panic.'[1]

Plenty of books have chronicled the causes and level of the current crisis in the Church of England. There is a loss of credibility about the whole enterprise not only from without, but also from within the Church. Some thinkers and watchers estimate that the fastest growing group of Christians in the West consists of those who no longer attend congregational forms of church. In my travels I have met some of these. Their belief in God and Christ seems intact. Some gather with fellow refugees in small groups to pursue spirituality and discipleship. For them congregational church life is simply no longer credible. Tell them Sunday attendance is church and they retort, 'I don't believe it.'

Other observers claim that half of those who still do go to Sunday congregational worship are hanging on out of a sense of duty.

John Drane[2] and others, like the Nottingham based researchers Hay and Hunt[3], have demonstrated that there is a double whammy over spirituality. While a rise in interest in spirituality is well documented, at the same time the Church is written off as merely religious and the the last place a spiritual seeker would go to. The second blow is that the Church is seen as a repressive force within modernism, one that has contributed to today's problems. If it is a cause, how can it possibly be part of the answer? So Mike Riddell can speak of the Church in the West as being like a dying patient who struggles, through denial and bargaining, to accept a terminal diagnosis[4].

## WHAT HOPE IS THERE OF CHANGE?

Back in March 1998, I attended a Learning Organisations Consultation Day at Holy Trinity, Brompton. It was one window on to the questions, 'Can the Church take on the characteristics of an adaptable and intelligent organism?' and, 'Can it learn how to change?' That day provided a microcosm of my own reflections over two decades of seeing the Church of England encounter challenges from an evolving mission context and the emergence of new expressions of church. I came away realising that the challenge of change is even harder than I had thought.

### Defensive structures

The Church of England comprises forty-three county-size organisations (the dioceses) that are themselves made up of between two hundred to five hundred separate units (parishes). The last external review of the Church of England, *To a Rebellious House*, called the dioceses 'a confederation of medieval feudal barons'[5]. Any important call for change by archbishops or General Synods is sieved through these two structural layers, and the most radical changes are quietly made safe. In most cases the only enforceable issues are legal and financial, through the canons and centralised finance system. Even then, however, there are cases of parishes refusing to pay the quota, many cases of the conduct of worship outside official liturgical provision and the holding of various beliefs in variance with the canons.

The independence of diocesan bishops and the freehold for clergy both make it impossible to compel or require change at the institutional level. The cost associated with disciplinary action (up to a quarter of a million pounds) and the negative publicity it always attracts, turning the prosecuted into martyrs, make that route as untenable as it is undesirable.

### Clergy with attitude?

There have been various attempts since the 1970s to move towards enabling collaborative ministries, both in the style of training at colleges and through various diocesan ministry schemes. Despite this, there are still many clergy who see themselves as generalists, competent in all areas, and many churches where the laity have assisting roles only, if they are allowed to do anything at all.

The Partners in Mission report cited the collusion of many laity in this plot: 'Many clergy fear lost of status by sharing their ministry with lay people and many lay people are prepared to let the clergy be the church.'[6] Out of fear and insecurity, these clergy are deeply resistant to change.

### The place of the parish

The national commitment to the parish system, though admirable in theory, too often in practice has meant that resources are being stretched too thinly. The search for substitute clergy in the face of the decline of stipendiary ministers has largely been driven by the belief that the parish system should be kept intact. It is even possible to argue that the moves towards OLM are but an attempt to find an ersatz substitute to staff the parish, as is the passion for the collaborative style, which recruits an unordained but clericalised strata of laity.

By contrast, the calls for complementary ways of pursuing our mission focus, and for recognising the reality of human networks that do not fit with parishes, were officially endorsed through the synodical acceptance in 1994 of a church planting report *Breaking New Ground*[7]. Its first chapter is still the clearest official rationale on that subject, but emerging writing on church for Generation X, youth congregations and internet based church develop this further. The language of network recognises that social identity may be formed distinct from place and without significant connection to place. The watchword is becoming, 'We must do our mission on the basis of how people live and can no longer do it on the basis of where they sleep.'

Yet any radical move away from the parish base is still seen in many quarters as an unthinkable betrayal of trust. The parish is also strongly linked to the presence of some 16,000 centres of Anglican worship, a good proportion of which are of architectural merit and have at least residual congregations. Wholesale church euthanasia is not top of the agenda and would be strongly resisted by both traditionalists on the inside and by the institutional fringe, who are still willing to pay in part for their church that they don't go to.

### Does democracy deliver?

The democratisation of the Church of England since the 1920s, leading by stages to its present synodical structures, also militates against radical change. It is not difficult to find a critical mass for change in some parishes and there are signs of similar changes at the level of bishops' staff meetings. It is far less easy, however, to command such forces for change at Deanery, Diocesan or General Synod. One, out of many, examples would be the length of time it took to move from the raising of the issue of the ordination of a woman during World War Two to the eventual passing of that legal measure amid enormous and on-going tensions. It is thus said by some that democratisation has led to emasculation. In a fast-changing society that is a severe disadvantage.

### Mission mistiness

The Church of England does not have, and possibly never has had, a consensus on what it means by mission. Though a model was provided by the Anglican Consultative Council in 1984 (ACC-6), and was subsequently added to in the 1990s with a timely clause about ecological concerns, these formulae do not seem to be widely known, recognised and used in the normal councils of the Church. There are still the old polarisations between evangelism and social action, between conversion to Christ and incorporation into the Church, and unresolved tensions between the relationship between the Church and the Kingdom. Thus to envisage any agreement about what it is to become a missionary congregation is hopeful at best. While it is true that there is increasing theological consensus that the Church is at heart missionary, the lack of consent on mission means that there is no agreement about what it is actually sent to do.

### The lessons of history

It is difficult to pinpoint any period in history when an established Church institution was able to renew its own inner life for mission. Rather it appears that new movements arose, to some extent, in discontinuity with the past. The necessity for this uncomfortable process is endorsed by Jesus' advocacy of 'new wineskins' (Matthew 9:17).

Examples of such discontinuity would be the founding of the monastic orders, then subsequently of the friars, the Wesleyan revival and the birth of the modern missionary movement. To some extent the Reformation is a further example of discontinuity, though its evangelistic impact was minimal. In our own day, the house churches and the basic ecclesial communities would be candidates. It is at least a matter of open conjecture whether, at the turn of the second millennium, amid the wealth of creativity in new expressions church, we are at a similar juncture again. I guess we shall have to dare to tolerate severe strains to unity in order to welcome the arrival of disturbing creativity.

> Another important consequence of the model of change through discontinuity is the vulnerability of the new movements. They can be subverted by their background institution, either by deliberate attack, or by the compromise of assimilation. They are also prey to the process of their own internal decay into becoming themselves fresh institutions. This in turn provokes the need for fresh movements to continue the ceaseless process of re-forming the Church.

### PENSIVE ABOUT THE POSITIVES

I remain unconvinced that the structures as a whole, and the majority of the present clergy, can be radically changed so that they become mission-minded. But there are some signs of life.

1.  Change is already coming piecemeal from the grassroots, encouraged and defended in many cases by pioneer spirits among episcopal staff

teams. These personal partnerships of trust are our best hope.

2. There are also some grounds of hope that revised training priorities will lead to mission-minded, forward thinking ordinands. But though the theological colleges have been claiming that for twenty-five years, their curricula grow fuller not simpler. The recasting of all theology in a mission framework is easier to talk about in theory than turn into practice.

3. The dioceses do have some mission resources to deploy on the ground. Episcopal staff teams by discretionary funds, growth and opportunities funds and discretionary posts, can make available seed corn finance to begin new mission-minded ventures. The deeper challenge is to sustain what has been seeded and our track record here is less impressive.

4. There is widening consensus that we cannot go on as we are – not least in terms of money available, clergy numbers and the credibility of the Church in its institutional guise. This opens a climate in which there is a readiness for change and in which calls such as the call for 'a decade of experimentation' can be made. My fear is that today's experiment is tomorrow's expendable.

• The life and profile of the new ventures create further possibilities of change. If it is true that new mission-minded ventures represent the values of the Kingdom invading the life of the Church, then it may be reasonable to suggest that these little local developments may have something of the power of the yeast to leaven the lump of dough. Yeast may be seen as a healthy subversive element, introduced into a wider somewhat inert body. It is a possible analogy of the way in which church planting and new expressions of church continue to change what is meant by Church.

### Oh dear!

I was part of a day devoted to the subject of change and the Church. I do not say that nobody thought it, but nobody mentioned as even a possible source of change in the wider Church of England, that people might have a life-changing encounter with a missionary God. The small cynical part of me wondered whether all this talk of changing the systems and structures was in danger of being little more than the Church doing its own equivalent of the recent secular reorganisation of the education system and the Health Service that have been so astonishingly expensive, exhausting and stressful without perhaps noticeably improving the quality of the product delivered either to children or patients.

## WHERE ARE THE SIGNS OF HOPE?

Some will rightly want to tell stories of effective mission and lasting renewal in existing churches. Others will turn to strategies such as those identified in the Springboard booklet *There Are Answers*[8] that have been shown to make a difference to local churches. I salute all these but at times I wonder if they are akin to signs of remission in a patient with a terminal disease.

### A changing landscape

Since the mid-1990s a whole variety of new expressions of being church have emerged. A call for the re-imagining of church has come partly from the disillusioned, but also from discoveries in mission, and these responses have thrown up new patterns and forms. It might be reduced to a pair of questions: 'What is the relationship between mission and church?' and, 'Which should shape which?' I am among some wanting to argue that in a post-Christian mission context, it will only be as Christians proceed in mission that they will discover what church should actually become. So for me these new ventures are the greatest signs of hope. Some are more radical than others, some more numerous, some more vulnerable. Let me sketch the picture by taking them in alphabetical order.

### 1. Alternative worship

The famous early example was the Nine o'Clock Service – NOS. Many subsequent events owe much to that creative style, though distancing themselves from all forms of abusive leadership. They seek to be responsive to postmodern culture, expressing preferences for ambiguity and antiquity. They represent a serious attempt to reinculturate worship and engage with preferences for a multi-media approach that may be diffuse or focused. Their style is created locally rather than remotely, works contextually rather than institutionally, makes use of the symbolic and the subversive rather than the didactic, and is open-ended. Their inner sense of community is strong, the worship highly creative. But outward facing mission is often weak, not least because their members are often in recovery from poor past experiences of church. They should not be thought of as youth churches as their age group is wider.

## 2. ArchTraditional

Examples would be new congregations formed around 1662 services, individuals preferring anonymous attendance at cathedrals, those seeking Roman Tridentine Mass celebrations or people converting to Greek or Russian Orthodoxy. Here, being relevant is seen only as the vice of marrying the spirit of the age. The model affirms the timelessness of Christian doctrine, ethics and liturgical practice reinforced by welcome familiarity. At its best, here is provision of stability in a vortex of change.

## 3. Building community

This is shorthand for beginning church through community development. It is a classification that I admit I have invented and popularised as a result of my research since 1999. These churches are found in areas of social deprivation but also of significant dislocation from existing forms of church. Sometimes the planting method has been intentional, appropriate to the level of social need and the mission context. Sometimes the forming of church has surprised a Christian group engaged in community development programmes. Community building in partnership seems the best way forward in working with the urban non-churched, who are suspicious of all overt churchly approaches.

## 4. Cell plants

Cell moves the heart of church from congregation to small group. There are two categories. In the first, it is believed that the value of attending these small groups is such that they replace traditional church attendance. It is held that all the major functions of church – worship, teaching, building community and engaging in mission – can take place in the cell. Cells exist to multiply. Cell plants are not transitions of existing churches to cell thinking but are church plants for non-churched people, set up from scratch with small teams.

The second cell category of planting new expressions of church is the creation of cell churches parallel to congregations. There is some evidence that cell makes church more effective in discipleship, lay ministry and evangelism. I am impressed that cell can be combined with almost any other of the models in my list.

### 5. Counter-cultural

These are existing churches whose rhetoric over their identity, shown in the chosen worship style, discipleship programme and evangelistic intention indicates that they repudiate significant elements of both secular and existing church culture, hence the label I have chosen. As such they are not totally unlike the renewal based churches of the 1970s. It remains to be seen whether, like the latter, they are assimilated back into the mainstream or whether they branch out in order to remain distinct. Another label for them could be tribal churches.

A difference from the 1970s times of renewal is that I sense that some of these groupings are testing out the lifeboats formed by their networks, for they suspect that the liner of the wider Church may have hit an iceberg. The appointment of Archbishop Rowan Williams will alarm them yet more, though my view is that his essential orthodoxy, deep spirituality, counter-cultural stance and practical commitment to mission are good gifts to the Church.

### 6. Congregational church plants

A decade ago up to forty of these were started every year, but the diversity of other ways means that today there are fewer new congregational church plants. When they conform to a stereotype, they are now regarded as 'traditional' plants. These fall within a parish and serve a geographical sub-unit of it. Led by a curate or lay reader, they take a small congregational team of, say twenty, find a secular building and offer informal services of a family service type. Concern has been expressed that too often planting has meant the cloning of churches that are failing or inappropriate. There may still, however, be large new areas of private housing in expanded villages and on the edges of towns that warrant this approach.

### 7. Midweek church

Depending on which figure is taken from Peter Brierley's *The Tide is Running*

*Out*, between 9 per cent and 12 per cent of church attendance occurs midweek[9]. Where these meetings serve groups of people who make them their main congregational service, they are more helpfully thought of as churches rather than just services.

Stories are emerging of increased recognition being given to midweek communions, midweek church for the elderly, lunchtime church for the business community and the creation of worship tailored to children and accompanying adults at the close of the school day. At times attendance can be as large as on a Sunday. Midweek church offers the opportunity to widen the diversity of church in a community.

### 8. Multiple congregations
Multiple congregations using one shared building are growing in popularity once more. It is debatable whether this is less difficult and less divisive than starting out in a fresh venue. I hope those involved will learn the lessons of the early 1990s, which show that where existing kinds of worship are doubled up merely as an administrative arrangement, the experiment does not last.

Elements that help give genuine identity to multiple congregations include: planned divergence of worship style, the provision of dedicated and recognised leadership, particularity in the chosen mission of differing congregations and the existence of discrete pastoral care structures for each congregation. There is some overlap in the midweek category and congregations could borrow from the philosophy of many of the other new expressions of church explained here.

### 9. Network churches
These churches are a significant departure from the inherited parochial pattern. Their commonality is their target group – that is, people who find their identity in networks rather than territory, but their divergence is in the models of church and mission style employed to reach these people. This ranges across cell, seeker, Vineyard and social engagement, with combinations across those choices. They are clearly distinguished from past eclectic churches in that by diocesan agreement, and often by legal entity, they have no parish territory for

which they are responsible. As such they raise sharp questions about the nature of Anglican existence and are a group of churches sparking great interest.

## 10. Seeker churches

This is the least clear category of new expressions of church. Some lack of clarity is inherent in that the philosophy of seeker churches is to provide Sunday presentation that is intentionally not like church. As such it is not a new expression of church, but a deliberate shunting of church into midweek events to provide worship, teaching and community building. It is creditable that seeker allows the needs of the outsider to shape the Sunday experience.

Some people are critical of seeker church as over-resource hungry and therefore as being only an option for existing large churches. The other criticisms are that it is better suited to Boomers than Gen X and worse, it panders to consumerism. Few totally new seeker churches have been started, rather, existing churches have begun an additional seeker event. This is similar to the provision of Alpha courses, which are usually not intended to become new churches.

## 11. Youth congregation

In my experience so far, these are more trumpeted than practised. There are notable examples, but at present it is difficult to discover whether there is a meaningful national network. I don't here include monthly, let alone quarterly, youth services. Rather, real youth congregations that have weekly patterns, recognised leaders, pastoral structures and internally set mission targets.
Increasing numbers recognise the validity of youth congregation as meeting a theological not just a strategic need. Some repudiate the concept as ageist and unhelpfully homogenous. On cultural grounds, however, a case may be put. Moreover, before criticising others, the existing Church, which as dominantly white, middle-class and female, should examine itself.

I have written about all these types of church, by telling particular stories and then reflecting more widely on their significance[10]. The list is not exhaustive. In a couple of years I will have to add paragraphs on missionary orders, household church, table fellowship and I know not what. That's why I stick to an evolving booklet series rather than trying to write a tome.

I don't pretend that these expressions of church are sweeping all before them. On an optimistic day, when they are all lumped together and a generous assessment is made of the number of examples, I calculate they only make up about seven per cent of the 16,000 Anglican congregations in this country. It is still a day of small things.

## WILL THE CHURCH MAKE IT?

### Opportunity and danger

The credibility crisis gives scope to imagine the future. So some can be positive and think we are being offered the most open chance for hundreds of years to re-imagine church. I dare to think this may be more radical than the Reformation, but I hope it will be less divisive. In the unfolding and uncertain process into which we are being propelled by circumstances, I note the words of an African Christian connected to the Community Transformation videos: 'Nothing will happen until you are desperate enough.'[11] I guess it is a gift, as well as a judgment of God, that the backdrop of our day is the Church's loss of credibility.

The parts of Scripture I turn to, which resonate with the turbulent days in which we live, were written for the eighth to sixth centuries BC. I expect exile for the Church as we have known her. I guess we shall have to learn how to sing the Lord's song in a foreign land. I encourage a counter-cultural existence for Christian communities.

Rather than revival, I am waiting for the death and resurrection of the Church. That is my estimation of the situation we face.

**Notes**

1 *The Times*, 3 June 2002.

2 John Drane, *The McDonaldisation of the Church*, DLT, 2000, pp. 5-7.

3 David Hay and Kate Hunt, *Understanding the spirituality of people who don't go to church, a report on the findings of the Adults' Spirituality Project*, University of Nottingham, 2000.

4 Mike Riddell, *Threshold of the Future*, SPCK, 1998, p.1.

[5] Church of England's Partners in Mission Consultation, *To a Rebellious House,* PIM, 1981, p 22.

[6] op. cit., p. 25.

[7] House of Bishops, *Breaking New Ground: Church Planting in the Church of England,* GS 1099, CHP, 1994.

[8] Robert Warren and Bob Jackson, *There are Answers,* Springboard Resource Paper, 2001.

[9] Peter Brierley, *The Tide is Running Out,* Christian Research, 2000, pp. 157-185.

[10] Readers can consult the website www.encountersontheedge.org.uk or contact Mrs Claire Dalpra, The Sheffield Centre, 50 Cavendish Street, Sheffield S3 7RZ, tel. 0114 2727451.

[11] *Transformations—A Documentary,* The Sheffield Group, 1999.

# 2. Can these bones live?

## TIM HUMPHREY

What steps can we take towards consensus among our parishioners on the current state of our Church, its relevance and potential?

Is it time for an honest admission to the lay person that the clergy do not hold all the answers on how to move forward – and that without ground level involvement (and subsequent taking of certain responsibilities) there will be no future for the Church?

*Tim Humphrey became the Vicar of St Barnabas Church, Kensington (an Holy Trinity Brompton Church plant) in 2002. When he wrote this chapter, he was still working for the Diocese of Winchester (as a faith development officer), and for the Warham Trust, which, coming from the evangelical-charismatic stream, is seeking to bring renewal to the church in rural north Hampshire, while evangelising the unreached.*

### INTRODUCTION

Four years ago I moved from suburbia, where I'd spent all my life, to just outside Basingstoke, to join the Winchester diocesan mission team. Before long I went to lead the Sunday services for a group of parishes just six miles from Basingstoke. Here I took the 8 a.m. service for eight people, the 9 a.m. (where the organist failed to arrive) for four people. At the next church, there was a 10.30 a.m. family service, which was in fact a 1662 sung Communion and the one child stayed in and talked all through.

> I found the day extremely depressing! I knew that typical rural parish church was probably quite different from a thriving church in London's commuter belt, but I hadn't realised how deeply I would have to re-think the issues around evangelism and renewal.

> Having now lived and worked in rural North Hampshire for five years, my concern has been for the many Christians who love their local

church, firmly believe it to be God's intended agent of mission in the parish, yet are disheartened and disillusioned. It may be that there is no provision for their children, inadequate teaching and worship that leaves them uninvolved and uninspired. They could never invite their friends to such a church. It may be that over many years they have tried to stay enthusiastic but have found their own faith and love ebbing away. Often these people want to know just one thing. Should they pull out and join another church or should they remain in the hope that renewal may yet come.

To take an entrenched view is probably unproductive as there can be no way of predicting what lies ahead in the life of any individual church. The fact is that long-established churches have ebbed and flowed from the beginning. Some have literally died, their buildings being sold and the remaining congregation dispersed. Others on the brink of closure have experienced a new lease of life.

## LEADERSHIP FOR RENEWAL

Studies into why churches experience renewal have identified several factors, but the overriding one would appear to be visionary leadership. With the call of God on a leader's life, the blessing and grace of God attend the ministry and new life and vision follow. To wait for an individual church to be renewed is usually a case of waiting for the appropriate leadership to emerge.

## COMMUNITY AND RENEWAL

But the purpose and effect of renewal is not just blessing a particular church or structure. It is the creation of a vibrant Christian community of faith in which believers are nourished, taught and enabled to use their various gifts to extend the mission of Christ. The prophet's vision in Ezekiel 37:1-14, the valley of dry bones, has rightly been read as an encouragement to God's people to reach out in faith for renewal when hope has almost been extinguished. Yet these bones represent 'the whole house of Israel' (verse 11) – those called to partake in Yahweh's covenant with his people and to witness to his glory. They do not represent the structure of Israel's pre-exilic government or even particular forms of cultic worship. God's intention in calling Israel was that by celebrating his covenant with him, they would be witnesses to his saving acts. In Ezekiel's context, the renewal of each individual was in order that *together* they might become an *army* for fulfilling God's purposes.

> In this context, it is not structures that are renewed but individuals who respond to the prophetic call of God. God will renew and restore his people, but not always the social, economic and religious structures surrounding earlier blessing.

## NEW STRUCTURES

Yet the structures and strategies accompanying the Church's mission and ministry are important if the new wine of the Spirit is to be contained and come to maturity. God gives new life and pours out his Spirit upon people, yet he somehow requires us to develop the structures that allow its sustaining and promote its effectiveness (Luke 5:37-38). It was said of the Wesley brothers that their success in the eighteenth century lay not only in their inspired preaching and the accompanying grace of God, but in their methodical structures for discipleship. By contrast, Whitefield, though many believed his preaching to have been more effective at the time, did little to provide adequate structured follow-up and much blessing was lost.

> The history of the Church has been of constant running to catch up with the Spirit of God as he has touched and equipped new and diverse groups of people, sometimes on the edges of the Church or even quite apart from it. The question then is not so much whether individual churches may experience renewal – most certainly they may, but whether current structures and strategies help or hinder in channelling the new wine of the Spirit and hence the formation of genuine Christian community.

## HOW CHRISTIAN COMMUNITIES ARE FORMED

Some (certainly the majority of traditional Anglican churches) arise out of the shared faith of those living within a particular geographical area (the parish). Others arise out of a shared common experience within a specific context (such as those churches arising out of a 'revival'), others from a desire to propagate a particular style of worship, ministry and theology, still others in order to engage a particular people-group. Within the current ecumenical spectrum, we can identify churches formed and re-formed around these factors.

## APOSTOLIC COMMUNITIES

There is another aspect of community that is worth noting. Many of the new forms of church now emerging are based on the principle of networks as opposed to territory. The traditional Anglican parish system was a way of dividing up the land for settlement and of ensuring consistency of ministry. It was appropriate because members of parishes had nearly all of their meaningful relationships within that one community. Here was a structure created on the basis of a missionary and pastoral imperative. Today, however, many people live their lives in networks. They gather around relationships, shared interests and common goals that do not necessarily, though they may, include a sense of belonging to the local community.

> This is a problem to an organisation that is based predominantly on a territorial, parochial structure. The challenge is that networks are proving highly effective in evangelism and ministry, and churches that acknowledge this are free to reach those people God has uniquely gifted them to reach.

> A network may be a group of people who meet at work through a Christian Union, at a lunchtime meeting in the city, or in a school prayer meeting. It may be an Alpha or Emmaus group that gains a life of its own quite outside the context of Sunday worship. For many, it is possible that such events, rooted in the context of their day-to-day lives, become as meaningful, and possibly more productive, than attendance at their own local church. The story of one man is telling:

> I spend more of my waking hours in the city than anywhere else. I meet more people in my office than I meet neighbours at home and have more opportunity to do good to those in my department than I do among my friends at home. Yet my church never prays for my work or the people I meet. Instead, I attend the midweek prayer meeting and pray for the women's coffee morning on Thursday. The lunchtime city meetings I attend are increasingly the place where I feel most at home with God.

The point is that God pours out his renewing Spirit in many and diverse situations. Where he does, community begins to form. The close guarding of parish boundaries (usually only by clergy – rarely the laity) may be a great hindrance to the developing of networks of relationships that gather around factors other than parochial proximity.

> An important feature in this landscape is the well-established tradition of religious communities, both residential and dispersed, that seek to create an environment in which God may be encountered and individual lives brought into discipleship. Here, a common rule provides not only a sense of identity but encourages its members to be proactive in their own ministries and, in the case of dispersed communities, in the life of their local churches. Christians in local churches have long looked to communities such as the Franciscan Third Order, Iona and Lee Abbey to resource and enrich their spiritual lives and have done so without seeing any conflict of interest. In this way alternative communities that transcend parochial or other structures provide for the renewing of individuals within their existing churches.

### THE WARHAM TRUST

My personal interest in alternative forms of Christian community has come through the development of the Warham Trust in North Hampshire. In the early 1990s a small group in the rural areas surrounding Basingstoke ran Alpha courses for their friends and neighbours without the direct support of any local churches. As the numbers increased, the problem of what to do with the new Christians became acute. It was recognised that many of the local rural churches were very small, serving equally small communities. Many were multi-parish benefices where several churches shared just one ordained minister who simply could not be regularly at any one service.

Stretched as these churches already were, they were often simply unable to provide the resources needed to sustain mission and growth or encourage those new to the Christian faith.

The Warham Trust was set up for the encouragement, renewal and training of laity. It seeks to build up members of the body of Christ in their local, often rural, churches both in North Hampshire and beyond. It does this by:

1. providing a supportive Christian fellowship;
2. training and developing the skills of lay people;
3. bringing others to faith;
4. encouraging and supporting the clergy;
5. responding to requests from parishes for particular training, courses or provision of teams to encourage local churches;
6. partnership in diocesan mission initiatives.

The Trust employs a missioner, and at the heart of the ministry is the Warham community. The community's role is to sustain and resource the Trust's work. It comprises those who feel called to support the work in practical ways and who are able and willing to contribute to the development of the community's life.

The Trust embraces a wide variety of people who identify with its aims and objectives and who look to the Trust in varying degrees for spiritual support and training. It operates a mailing list through which details of midweek training courses and open fellowship evenings and other events are advertised. The missioner is in frequent demand to assist parishes in the setting up and running of Alpha, Emmaus and other courses in which members of the community become involved.

### THE FUTURE

Those wrestling with the dilemma of whether to remain in their currently unproductive churches or to go elsewhere should at least seek a community where they can encounter God's presence and be nurtured and encouraged. It is neither helpful, nor necessary, to 'wait for renewal' while their own vision and passion suffer. No one can promise renewal for a particular church, but the Spirit is given to all who ask for him. It is hard to see how those who seek alternative churches or structures can be doing wrong and it seems likely that considerable numbers of existing churches within the Anglican system will simply not survive the rapidly aging congregations who support them. Of course, those who decide to remain in their existing churches can do much. They should not worry about trying to change the whole structure, but focus on an area of ministry in which they are gifted and called, and can gain permission to contribute. The challenge for these people is not to hinder the formation of alternative communities that they might perceive as a threat to their own convictions.

> In reality it may well be that we shall see an extension of the principal already noted, that for years people have resourced their spiritual lives from a *variety* of places or communities. The church down the road may not be the most effective group for mission and ministry, but this may matter less and less in the long run. As people are freed, encouraged and trained to be effective in exercising their own ministries and gifts, they will find sustenance wherever they can, while possibly remaining committed to a local church 'waiting for renewal'.

# 3. The pain and potential in change

## JAMES NEWCOME

A re we truly prepared to lead by example in seeking to tamper with the status quo and for the toll it may take in order to effect change? In our attempts to make the life of the church more accessible and relevant to our local communities, how do we move from an intrinsically organisational culture to one which prioritises relationships above all else?

*James Newcome became Bishop of Penrith in 2002, having worked for the Diocese of Chester for several years as their Director of Ministry.*

*This chapter goes beyond looking at the situation we face to suggest some possible alternatives to the dominant parish system.*

### PROBLEM

Talking recently to Robert Warren (one of our most perceptive thinkers about ministry and mission) I was very struck by an analogy he produced for the current state of the Church of England. He said it is rather like a container lorry. The container is the institution, fully loaded with centuries of tradition, thousands of buildings and the dead weight of bureaucracy. The two sets of wheels are our congregations and clergy. The size of the container has remained unchanged, but the wheel base is rapidly contracting. Our congregations, for example, are now below 1 million compared with 5.4 million in 1979[1]. If present trends continue, less than 1 per cent of the population will be attending church by 2016. Commentators suggest that England is now one of the most secular countries in the world.

At the same time, over the last thirty years there has been a 30 per cent decrease in the numbers of stipendiary clergy: 15,000 has come down to 10,000, and without women priests we would now be less than

8,000. In 1978 (the year I was ordained) General Synod accepted a report indicating that 11,600 full-time clergy was the minimum number required to staff the parochial system. We now have 2,000 fewer than that. And as Robert Warren points out, as the wheel base diminishes, the container becomes increasingly unstable – to a point where eventually even a small puff of wind could blow it over.

There is an equally striking image in Michael Riddell's book *Threshold of the Future*[2]. Michael Riddell, who comes from New Zealand, describes the way in which white ants attack a timber frame house. Apparently they eat the frame from the inside out. Everything looks fine for a while, but the structure becomes fundamentally unstable, to a point where one day it collapses.

The Cardinal Archbishop of Westminster recently referred to Christianity in this country as almost 'vanquished' and in 1998 the Archbishop of Canterbury commented at a conference in Harare, 'In some sections of our Western Church we are bleeding to death.' I recently attended a conference, 'Leadership for a Change', laid on by the Edward King Institute. One of the main speakers was John Drane, author of *The McDonaldisation of the Church*[3], and he made no bones about the fact that the Church of England is in a really serious state. His comments echoed the results of the National Listening Survey in 2001. Those interviewed likened the Church to a mole – 'mostly underground and in the dark, occasionally coming up for air, and when it does making a lot of mess in the process'!

Of course, the picture is not all doom and gloom! There are many rays of light, and the commitment and enthusiasm of those who remain is often extremely heartening. Some of our churches (especially the smaller ones) are growing and some of our clergy are exceptional.

However, it is easy for those of us who have any kind of responsibility in the Church of England to go into a state of denial about current trends and argue that if we only batten down the hatches tight enough it will all be all right in the end. Peter Brierley disagrees. 'If we don't change,' he says 'we won't be here to change in twenty years' time.' His words were echoed in *The Times* by Bill Ind, who is Bishop of Truro. Truro Diocese is in the process of cutting the number of its stipendiary clergy by 33 per cent and he remarked, 'A fundamental change to our patterns of ministry is needed... and unless changes are made, the institutional church as we know it will not survive.'

We need to change, and we must change now before it is too late. As long ago as 1983 John Tiller (who was then Chief Secretary of the Advisory Council for the Churches Ministry) wrote a prophetic report making the same point. It was duly shelved, and the options open to us have been decreasing daily ever since. We need to take note of the so-called 'product cycle' in industry. This suggests that every company needs regularly to reinvent itself, in the sense that it needs to put new products on the market, and it is essential that new products begin to supersede the old before the sale of the old ones has declined too far. In our case the basic product – which is the gospel – is the same, but the packaging, presentation, marketing and infrastructure have got to change. The Church needs to ask Charles Handy's pertinent question: 'If we didn't exist, would we recreate ourselves? If so, what would the new creation look like?' So – what's to be done?

## PRINCIPLE

The chief principle underlying any change to the structures of the Church of England should be transformation.

This means first of all *the transformation of individuals*. That is at the heart of what the Kingdom of God is all about, and throughout this discussion the Kingdom must remain our ultimate aim and goal. Scripture seems to suggest that God wants everyone to know him in Christ and witness to the gospel, so any patterns of ministry we may develop in the future must bear that in mind and contribute to bringing it about.

Second, there is *the transformation of leadership*. We need transformational leaders (whose training also needs to be transformational). That hasn't always been the case with the Anglican ministry, but things are changing, and patterns of leadership are rapidly becoming far more collaborative and inspirational. Like new music, collaborative leadership no longer belongs to any one tradition and we are all discovering that:

- bishops need to become more apostolic (actually taking initiatives and giving a lead, not just blessing the successes of others);
- clergy need to become more episcopal;
- lay people need to become more priestly (which does not mean more clerical!).

The key quality required in tomorrow's leaders is the ability to trust others (cf. Gillian Stamp's tripod: tasking, trusting, tending).

Third, there is *the transformation of the structures*. As we all know, structures are vital as a means of helping or hindering effective leadership and church growth. One 'enabling structure' that has emerged in recent years and is partly a product of the Decade of Evangelism is 'network evangelism'. This involves a recognition of the fact that nowadays the best way to reach people with the gospel is often through existing networks – at work, in leisure centres, in shops, on the internet, and wherever and whenever like-minded people congregate.

At the same time, we have become increasingly aware of the fact that some of our most cherished traditional structures actually now disable the Church's mission and ministry more than they promote it. These include:

- buildings – some are still a great sign of hope, but they become the opposite when they are cold, empty and crumbling. Some of our buildings are now a major millstone, sapping huge amounts of time, energy and money. There are far too many of them, and far too many of those are far too big and also inappropriate for worship in the twenty-first century;

- freehold – this is in some respects an albatross round the neck of the Church of England. It is certainly the enemy of any idea of compulsory continuing ministerial education; appraisal with a cutting edge; and dismissal of the incompetent;
- the parochial system – this is the most controversial. Many still regard the parochial system as the Church's great strength, desperately (and vainly) pleading for 'a priest in every parish'. But is it really a great strength or a great hindrance? Until recently I had always assumed the former. I am now beginning to think that it can on occasions be the latter, because, in Robert Warren's terms, the parish system is geared more to pastoral mode than mission mode (in other words, maintaining a status quo that can and should no longer be maintained). It should still be possible to retain an Anglican sense of responsibility for mission to the whole country without perpetuating an unworkable burden, irrelevant boundaries, and totally unrealistic expectations.

Finally, there needs to be *the transformation of community*. *Koinonia* is central to the whole discussion, though no longer always necessarily geographical. Currently, parish communities are devastated by 'occasional attendance' patterns. A lack of commitment to God, church and each other has its own severe effect on the quality of worship. A radical Christian community with vibrant, prayerful spirituality has to be the most powerful tool there is for mission in this country. The question is how to create such communities at the beginning of the twenty-first century.

## PRACTICE

Let me suggest an ideal scenario. This might consist of:
- Mission units replacing parishes and deaneries. The size of these would vary, but many would be about the size of a current large team or half a deanery.
- Local 'cells' scattered throughout the mission unit and geared for pastoral care, teaching and evangelism. These cells would constantly multiply. Each cell would have its own local leadership, which would probably be lay and definitely unpaid and invariably shared.

- A full-time staff team resourcing each mission unit. This team would consist of lay and ordained, mostly stipendiary, with various specialities and a team leader. Responsibilities would include the training and equipping of cell leaders and zone pastors.
- Large central buildings ('minster model') would remain for celebrations and main acts of worship.
- Bishops with an apostolic and strategic role would look after several mission units. There would be some 'senior' bishops but we would abolish the current diocesan/suffragan distinction.
- A permanent diaconate would be rediscovered, especially for coordinating and catalysing ministry on the boundaries of the church and community.
- Training resource centres for all types of ministry would be set up in place of theological colleges. These would focus on formation through apprenticeship and development of community. People with real theological expertise and gifts would gain theological qualifications through universities (including by extension).
- Accredited ministers would be authorised to preside at the Eucharist, but this would be very different from simply ordaining 'ordained local ministers' to plug sacramental gaps in parishes. There would be regular large central eucharistic celebrations in the big minster churches.

In order to implement such a strategy, we could begin by declaring a number of 'areas of experiment' (cf. local ecumenical projects), recognising that 'one size will not fit all' and different structures will suit different needs. We certainly need to value what has gone before and let the old coexist for a while. There is no need to unchurch anybody, but many parish churches will simply die. Instead of desperate attempts at resuscitation we need to transform them and think creatively about varied community use for many of our existing buildings. It may well be that it will be appropriate to retain some of our parishes as mission units and it will probably be many years before a new system takes over completely.

The main resistance to new patterns (whether these or others) will almost certainly be emotional and stem from vested interests. A process of this kind, however, is already beginning in Durham Diocese with its 'localities' and also in St Edmundsbury and Ipswich with its 'collaborative clusters'.

We are already adapting to survive, but much more adaptation is required if we are really to grow.

**Notes**

[1] See Peter Brierley, *The Tide is Running Out*, Christian Research, 2000.

[2] Michael Riddell, *Threshold of the Future*, SPCK, 1998.

[3] John Drane, *The McDonaldisation of the Church*, DLT, 2000.

## PART TWO

# SOME WAYS
# AHEAD

### SACRED TIME AND SPACE

Sacred time and sacred space is mine
to use to further grace. Space of ancient church
or just a niche among the Abbey choir
while chanting from the Psalter.

Time is mine, past and future miles apart –
the present time – time today to make a start
the nomads and the Hebrews wandered all about
their temples burnt – a space in time was won.

Sacred space was gone and sacred time took on
worship changed – *chronos* time is here –
*kairos* time we seek. Spirit's grace needs time
and space and as I ponder on my needs,
candle lit he my spirit feeds.

*Anna Newton*

LOOKING BACK TO LOOK FORWARD

LEARNING FROM ABROAD

SHARING GOOD PRACTICE

A CHALLENGE

# 4. Celtic inspiration for today[1]

## RAY SIMPSON

Simpson talks of sixth-century churches as being 'seven-days-a-week hubs of their society. How relevant to our local situation is our current church activity?**

**Are we still too comfortable, too infected by the society in which we live, to recognise any hunger to fulfil God's plan for his Church?**

*Ray Simpson is the Guardian of the Community of Aidan and Hilda (www.aidan.org.uk), and the author of many books on Celtic Christian spirituality and church forms. Here he suggests ways in which we might learn from the experience of the Celtic churches of the first millennium.*

The Church of England is in danger of losing the plot. It is not operating at the place where people perceive their spiritual needs to be. This fact is reflected in the statistics of decline.

There are three ways of responding to this crisis:

1. to resist change and wither away;
2. to manage change and decline efficiently – most dioceses are now doing this;
3. to allow what is in the heart of God for his Church at this time to come to birth. This requires a transformation in parish spirituality.

The size of this challenge was highlighted for me when I arrived at a London conference centre. The receptionist knew only two things about me: 'Church of England' and 'Celtic spirituality'. Her opening words were, 'It is in my genes to listen to intuition and dreams, but there is nothing in the Anglican tradition that does this. If I want to be in the Church of England I have to ignore this.'

Does she? Or can we harness the latent spirituality in her and in millions like her for a great renewal of Church and society? If we are to do this, we have to face the fact that humanity is going through a massive shift in its mental framework.

> The traces of Constantine's Church would seem to be fading, and a
> turning point as fundamental as the Constantinian one confronts us.
> *Cardinal Franz Konig*

Living churches heed Jesus' advice to understand the context of their time – you can tell the season by looking at the trees (Mark 13:28-29).

The vast paradigm shift that is needed means that the form church has taken in the West for centuries now needs fundamental reappraisal. This form, in both its Roman and Reformed varieties, is sometimes termed the Imperial model, because it imitates the top-down, one-shape-fits-all model that the Church borrowed from the Roman Empire's civil service. Now this has reached the end of its shelf-life. Second millennium church streams have tell-tale signs of a mind-set that is becoming obsolete. Even if we realise this is true, however, we may feel unable to move out of the framework we are stuck with.

We can take heart from the example of Christians in post Roman Britain and in Ireland whose culture in some respects resembled ours. Ireland was the first country to be evangelised that lay outside the Roman Empire. Thus a different way of being church emerged there. And what kept the Church together and enabled it to bring a fresh cradling of Christianity in lands within the Empire where Roman order had crumbled was the Irish people's monastic movement.

We need to look at what that Celtic movement has to offer us. This alternative model has been described as 'the house that John built' because John, perhaps more than any other apostle, modelled church as a large household of unconditional love. Inspired by a vision of the risen Christ, he wrote letters to seven churches (Revelation chapters 2–3) and discipled faith communities living in the area now known as Turkey, some of whose leaders, such as Bishop Irenaeus, came to Gaul.

Celtic churches felt a rapport with John, and with alternative churches that grew up in the deserts, because these were based less on regulation (as in the civil service model in the Latin part of the Roman Empire) and more on relationships. At their heart was a holiness that freed people to be themselves

> From the sixth century the Irish churches, inspired by this vision, became people's monasteries that turned Ireland into 'a land of saints and scholars'. These were then exported to the English.

These monasteries were seven-day-a-week hubs of their society. They served as prayer base, drop-in centre, library, school, health centre. They offered soul friends, training, entertainment and work to local people. To them visitors brought the news of the world.

People's monastery churches were completely open to the world. They were not enclosed as were continental monasteries, which had the 'us and them' mentality that Protestants later rejected. In Celtic monasteries children, housewives, farm workers and visitors would wander in and out and worship together.

The major Celtic monasteries were built on the main highways of sea and river in order to penetrate the population. Others grew, unplanned, out of places of spiritual retreat. There is need for both types of church today.

Irish churches introduced reading and writing to the people. Many druids and bards received this new gift of learning with open arms. Christianity had something to give that the people wanted.

Members of these churches regarded their founders as spiritual fathers or mothers whose authority lay in the mutual obligations of love. Yet they continued to have bishops living with them who were consecrated by bishops from the wider Church. Emerging churches need to express this twin principle of home-grown leaders and a link with wider Church leadership.

Celtic monastic church buildings were expendable and expandable. They consisted of wooden huts and meeting places that could easily be dismantled or added to.

There was diversity – each monastery church had its own flavour in worship and values (Rule) yet each was connected with the whole Church through common practices such as prayer, fasting, forgiveness, giving to the poor, keeping the Christian festivals, pilgrimaging to the world Christian centres, and the apostolic succession through ordination.

We cannot, and should not, copy the past – that is archaism – but we can draw inspiration from the past, and apply some principles in a way that brings transformation to Church and society today.

## THE POSTMODERN PARADIGM

Certain features of the postmodern paradigm signify the death of the Imperial form of church, and also lend themselves to a way of being church that resonates with Celtic models. Features of the postmodern paradigm that lend themselves to Celtic models of church are:

### 1. Relational rather than hierarchical

Postmodernism first appeared in architecture as a reaction to the dehumanising tower blocks of the 1960s. Postmoderns are suspicious of the mainstream in any area of life. An article by Francis Fukuyama in the *Financial Times* was headed 'The death of hierarchy'. Fukuyama argues that the flow of information is changing authoritarian forms of organisation in the workplace. They are being replaced by flat or networked organisations where shared values are the key[2]. Postmoderns are drawn to marginalised people because they do not impose hidden agendas. Postmoderns want to humanise the world; they are relationship centred.

In practical terms, this means that we give the building of relationships a higher priority than the maintaining of structures and buildings.

## 2. Spiritual rather than rational

Postmoderns love the spiritual. They delight in mystery and paradox. They are credulous, and love to hear stories of the miraculous. They do not need the resurrection of Christ to be proved to them.

The feminisation of society means that feelings have now won proper public respect alongside rationality. Sign, symbol and intuition are seen to be essential to explain the whole dimension of reality. These need to be embraced, though negative aspects of feminisation such as gender confusion, crisis in masculinity and denial of motherhood, also need to be addressed. Do people out there perceive the Church to be male, old, and left-brain dominated?

This change in what people seek has reached deep even into the young Evangelical world. According to Wheaton College professor Gary Burge: 'Say "liturgy" and my evangelical students have a reflex action akin to an invitation to do a quiz; say "mysticism" and they are drawn, fascinated, eager to see what I mean.'[3]

St Patrick recounts mystical experiences, which he sees as a fulfilment of Joel's prophecy, and the Celtic saints combine the practical and the mystical in a compelling way.

## 3. Explorative rather than possessive

Postmoderns dislike boundaries. To travel is more important than to arrive. To explore is okay, to package or market what you have found is not. Postmoderns distrust progress, are allergic to advertising, refuse to judge. Postmoderns don't want someone who knows it all. They want soul friends.

We should frequently recall that the leader of our Church is Jesus Christ who called himself 'the Way' (John 14:6). In the Acts of the Apostles people nicknamed church members those 'who belonged to the Way'(Acts 9:1-2). The Church, reflecting its members, gave the impression of being on a journey, on a voyage of discovery with God. Over the centuries the Church has accumulated buildings, structures, and mind-sets that focus on maintaining what it has, rather than on moving on with God. If our leader is 'the way', the Church must be more like a tent than a terminus.

Brother Roger, prior of the French community church at Taizé, refused the gift of a house because, he said, 'It makes everything so complicated.' His church is committed to 'the pilgrimage of trust on earth'. Even their worship building can expand or contract according to changing numbers.
In order to be an exploring person and church we build into our personal and church routines times of silence, listening and responding.

### 4. Inclusive rather than exclusive
Postmoderns like to draw out the possibilities that lie within everyone rather than to judge or pigeonhole them. The Church of England has talked much about its role as a 'comprehensive'

Church. Unfortunately many people thought this meant that the Church stood for anything or nothing and they despised it.

Yet within this concept is a God-given seed. This seed is hospitality. Hospitality can bind all sections of the Church in a common vision. It means welcoming all people as they are, until they feel able to bring their needs to the Church and to its God. It means not putting upon them alien requirements, but providing welcoming space and affirming presence in which they may journey.

The Bible calls us to be communities of hospitality. In the Gospels, a meal is the focus for much of Jesus' ministry. The first household churches ate together (Acts 2:46) and were told that some who had given hospitality to strangers had welcomed angels without realising it (Hebrews 13:2).

Early community churches in Britain and Ireland outgrew houses, but they still shared meals together and with strangers. They built refectories and one or several community members were set aside for the work of hospitality. Columba's community church at Derry fed a thousand hungry people daily. Even when David's monks in Wales ate only bread, they cooked appetising meals for the elderly and frail!

David's monks built friendly relations with those who lived around, used popular cultural idioms, and hosted the 'karaokes' of those days. Their best leaders took the trouble to share their faith with forgotten and foreign groups. They could do this because they were earthed in communities that freed them for this work, and that welcomed promising converts for training.

In the second millennium, most churches were praying places but not eating or sleeping places. In the twenty-first century, church buildings that are only the first tend to be ignored or vandalised. Although in a welfare state there is not always a physical need for churches to be eating places, there may be a social need. Sir Terence Conran, the restauranteur, predicts the emergence of the café society: 'Cafés will increasingly serve as outside offices and public spaces in which to do business.'

A small but increasing number of churches now provide cafés, lunch clubs, soup kitchens, DIY refreshment facilities, cabaret worship, or picnic areas. Emerging churches will provide back-packers' hostels, residential units built on to the main worship buildings, hermitages, linked housing schemes, cooperatives that enable members to buy houses nearby, night shelters and information on church websites on B&B provision in members' homes.

Anglicans have a reputation for cultural aloofness and elitism, for despising ways that lack aesthetic excellence, whether it be happy-clappy worship or ethnic bands. We can be perceived as introverted, lukewarm, incomprehensible and inhospitable. To encourage the life of God in those of different cultures from ourselves, to release them and give them opportunity – that is hospitality; to make space for groups so that they find and embrace the true and eternal love – that is what it means to be a comprehensive Church.

## 5. Culture friendly rather than anachronistic
The well-known mission sociologist David Bosch claims, 'The Christian faith never exists except as "translated" into culture.'[4] In order to baptise our culture we have to see it from the inside as does God.

Postmodern religion is *à la carte*. People select the ingredients with which they feel most comfortable. Churches that do not provide for this become obsolete. Emerging churches have a heart for the people, and are therefore willing to go with the flow of their lives.

The Church can relate to the culture in which it is set in four ways:

> absorption – this happens when Christians have handed over the Church's soul to the prevailing culture;
> rejection – this leads to Fortress Church, which becomes a monument;
> take-over – often the second millennium Church has done this;
> transformation from within. This is the way of Jesus, the Celtic Church, and must be the way of the emerging Church.

Jesus was able to become one with the people in all things except sin because he remained one with his divine Father at all times. Because he was secure, he did not pressurise others. He was able within himself to lose earthly power, and so became King of hearts. His critics, the Pharisees, had big evangelistic campaigns, and would traverse the earth to gain one convert, but failed to turn round the hearts of the people. Why? They imposed their culture on the people, whereas Jesus made himself one with them.

The early church of Jerusalem understood Christ to be fulfilling the God-given elements in the Jewish religion. As Christianity spread to non-Jewish cultures, Church leaders, too, portrayed Christ as the fulfilment of their truest insights. The apostle John went East and helped Greek-speaking seekers to recognise Christ as the *Logos* (Life Force) who sheds light on every person who comes into the world (John 1:9).

In Celtic Christianity true evangelism begins within the culture and flows out of love for the whole person. It grows out of relationships. It gives God and people time and space. It is natural.

In Celtic mission there are three elements:

1. good news to share;

2. modelling this good news through churches that help the needy, motivate seekers and offer ceaseless prayer;
3. a fellow feeling for others that enables the Christian to get inside their skin. Without all three elements mission fails.

In his book *How the Irish saved civilisation*[5], Thomas Cahill describes how St Patrick swam into the hearts and imaginations of people. They felt good about him. He started where they were. He used their language. This is in fact only doing on a small scale what Jesus did on the grand scale in his incarnation. It is doing what St Paul did: 'When with the Gentiles I live as a Gentile' (1 Corinthians 9:21). It is the spirituality of the shoes. We put ourselves in the shoes of the other.

> Lord, help me to walk in the boots of the miner,
> the shoes of the trader,
> the moccasins of the trapper
> and the sandals of Jesus the Master.
>
> *Native American prayer*

The Celtic Christian pioneers brought the life of Christ into the natural patterns of the people, they did not hoist individuals out of their patterns and give them a private religion.

We, who for the first time since those days live in a predominantly pagan population, do well to learn from the Celtic Christians, who in effect said to their pagan contemporaries: 'Come with your festivals that celebrate the elements, and we will transform them into festivals for the Lord of the elements. Come with your long flowing hairstyles – when we become Christian monks we will keep these hairstyles because they give glory to God. Come with your clans and natural networks of association, and we will plant Christian communities of prayer that go with the grain of these networks. Come with your excitement about the after-world, but let us see how the risen Son of God throws light upon it. Come with your hunger for worship and the world of the Spirit, and we will explain how idols have no place now, because the God of gods has revealed himself to us.'

Celtic Christians met at the people's natural gathering places. Some significant gathering places today are cafés, pubs, parks, leisure centres, schools, shopping centres, health centres, airports.

Only a minority now follow mainstream religion, but the Alister Hardy Research Unit has discovered that nearly two-thirds of the British population admit to having religious experiences. The emerging Church listens to this reservoir of spirituality and draws from its own reservoir things that will provide nourishment.

## 6. Holistic rather than fragmented
The Bible has a holistic world view. The second millennium Church lost this. The emerging Church will recover it or disintegrate.

In Christ, the head of the Church, all things hold together (Colossians 1:17-18). Outside of Christ all things fall apart. Primal, ecological and New Age spiritualities recognise that we are all connected to the web of life, but often this is not seen by the churches.

The Enlightenment years split off the mind from the body, science from religion, money from morality, the sacred from the secular, and Christians from the universal Church. Postmoderns are done with this. They know that the earth is a connected biosphere, that human beings are bound up with the web of life. Generation X is fed up with fragmented Christianity. Christians no longer want to be defined by a protest movement of four hundred years ago called the Reformation.

Millennium two churches became disconnected from the grass roots' patterns of the people, from the communal memory and from the earth itself. A minister told me, 'I have no problem in getting more people to come to church. We have good numbers attending our Alpha courses, and social events. What we lack is something deeper, something that gives us all a sense of belonging, and enables us to connect at every level.'

Yet young as well as old clergy think of themselves first as 'Evangelicals',

'Reform', 'Catholics', 'Forward in Faith', 'liberals', 'post evangelicals' or 'charismatics', as Anglican second, and as part of the one Church third. It is the disease that Paul warned against: 'When some of you say, "I belong to Paul's group", and others say, "I belong to Apollo" group", don't you realise you are behaving like non-Christians?' (1 Corinthians 3:4). I meet ex Anglicans who have become Orthodox and they say that is one reason why they have converted. They realise, and so must thoughtful Anglicans realise, that the Church, if it is to be true and deeply Christian, must have the homogeneity of the Body of Christ, and styles, symbols, are secondary. As people go deeper and to the Centre, their churchmanship style is also deepened, changed and becomes homogeneous.

We need to reconnect science with God, money with morality, the secular with the sacred, sexuality with the spirit, individual choice with justice, doctrine with experience. As churches do this, they will be honed to take on bigger tasks: to re-ensoul the world. Emerging churches will provide prayers and presences to help people mark a birth or anniversary, a new home, job or relationship, to bless or draw forth potential in places, schools, research, industry, commerce and leisure.

Emerging churches seek to offer their little plans in relation to the bigger whole, to what God is doing in the world at large. Like Marylebone Church, which is part and parcel of a multi-faceted healing centre, they seek to join up again that which has been fragmented.

### 7. Earth- rather than ego-centred

Ecological awareness is on the increase. Respected experts believe that the earth in its present form will not survive unless the fast expanding human race radically changes longstanding selfish habits. People who seek the good of the earth seek something that God desires, yet few perceive churches to be allies. Many of these people recognise that to befriend the earth requires spirituality, yet few of them find creation-friendly spirituality in the churches. Many people seek a spirituality which is natural, and they feel violated if the Church puts on unnatural airs, or neglects the earth.

The Bible's record of God's saving acts is set in the framework of God creating everything (Genesis 1 and 2). God named the first man Earth (*Adamah*). Mr Earth's first act was to name, and thereby bless, each of earth's creatures (Genesis 2:19). Jesus Christ, whom St Paul names 'the second Adam', meaning 'the second Mr Earth' (1 Corinthians 15:47), comes from heaven, yet contains within his humanity the whole evolving earth story, and its groaning in anticipation of its coming total fulfilment (Romans 8:19-23).

Spiritual thirst draws many towards earth-based spiritualities. Because Celtic Christianity grew in the ferment of a nature religion it retained a soul-deep appreciation of the earth, whereas other expressions of Christianity dismissed the material world as fallen and therefore as worthless.

> My church teaches me to be reconciled to God and to people, but it does not teach me to be reconciled to the earth.
>
> *Catherine*

To be creation friendly does not mean that we don't take sin or Jesus seriously. The Bible teaches us to be creation friendly. This creation friendly theology continues to this day in the Eastern Church but in Western churches an earth-denying theology took over. Spirit was divorced from matter.

Celtic churches in the West did not lose a creation friendly understanding. 'Augustine taught that creation was an act of God's power, Celtic Christians saw it as an act of God's love' (Lesslie Newbiggin). Columbanus, echoing St Paul in Romans 1:20, taught church members to live with two books in their hands: the Scriptures and creation.

Emerging churches can be friends of the earth by incorporating creation in their teaching, their worship and their lifestyle. Habitual celebration of the earth as an expression of God's life should include songs, signs and prayers, beautifying and energising meeting places with plants, signs or paintings of creation. Each week members may bring tokens of creation and explain the ways in which these speak to them of God. The earth and animals are often blessed; sunrise, solstice and prayer walks are held.

Emerging churches, like the Jews, mark the seasons. They use energy saving, non-polluting materials, recycled products, buy local, fair trade or organic foodstuffs, donate to ecology projects, improve the ecology of their area, build up eco consciousness in local schools, support local ecology groups or the Agenda 21 Process initiated by the Rio Earth Summit of 1994. They get out into the outdoors, cut out over-consumption, and practise forgiveness. They observe a day of rest on Saturday or Sunday – for example, by being together instead of all travelling in different directions. They make the best of any cur-tilage, churchyard or garden area: for wild flowers, growth of fruits or vegetables. They create connections with wild places, reclaim and guard sacred spaces.

Emerging churches create water features (early Christian churches had foun-tains flowing by their baptisteries) and creation theme corners, thus bringing together the feminine (wells) with the masculine (square buildings).

They make peace gardens and jogging tracks in the locality . They keep allot-ments and share the produce.

## CONCLUSION

These seven changes that the new paradigm enjoins require of us a funda-mental reappraisal of attitudes and practices. It is nothing less than a re-for-mation.

It will not come about unless we embrace a deep *metanoia*, a transforming repentance. Those who are able to engage in this will be those who are will-ing to go into the desert. The new paradigm calls us to adopt desert spiritu-ality, to create regular spaces for silence, examination and transparent accountability to an anamchara (soul friend or mentor).

Recent scholarship concludes that the Lindisfarne Gospels are more than great art, they are a kind of first manifesto of the English Church, written by monastic scribes who used their pens to bring life. The Gospels were dedi-cated to St Cuthbert, who was the first great native leader of the Anglo Saxon Church in the largest English kingdom. In producing these Gospels,

Lindisfarne and other main centres of English Christianity were coming together to make a statement: that the English Church combined both Celtic and Roman traditions and was a distinctive and fully integrated part of the universal Church.

Three passages are embroidered uniquely in the Lindisfarne Gospels: the Beatitudes; the father's welcome of the lost child; and Christ's wilderness struggle with temptations. It is thought that these were chosen to illustrate three peaks of Cuthbert's – and of the new English – spirituality. They may be taken to represent a church lifestyle of gentle simplicity as lived in the early monastic churches; of hospitality and welcome towards those outside as well as inside the Church; and discernment of spirits and overcoming of evil with good.

It is the birthright of the Church in this land, a birthright that only now is to come to full flower.

---

**Notes**

[1]  This chapter is based on the paper prepared for the Symposium at St Deiniols, September 2001.

[2]  *Weekend Financial Times*, 12/13 June 1999.

[3]  *Christianity Today*, 6 October 1997.

[4]  David Bosch, *Transforming Mission: Paradigm Shifts in Theology of Mission*, Orbis Books, Maryknoll, New York, 1991.

[5]  Thomas Cahill, *How the Irish saved civilisation*, Doubleday, 1995.

# 5. A missionary Church in Britain

## TIM DAKIN

With our identity tied up in the 'certainties' of the past, how do we isolate what is of relevance to the rapidly changing nature of the Church?

In our capacity as leaders, how do we create a balance between the theology of presence and the theology of performance?

*Tim Dakin was born in Mpwapwa, Tanzania, to parents who were mission partners with the Church Army. Before becoming General Secretary of CMS, he was Principal of Carlile College, Nairobi.*

*In this chapter Tim draws on Henry Venn's three-self policy for the church (self-supporting, self-governing and self-extending) to explore how this approach might help the Church of England today.*

In this chapter, based on my J. C. Jones Memorial Lecture 2001, I begin by briefly reviewing one of the principles inherited as part of the legacy of the Venn (John and Henry) mission leadership. I focus on the church principle and critically explore how this principle was worked out in CMS mission strategy, in its foundations, three-self policy and outreach to 'regions beyond'. I conclude by reviewing the patterns – the grammar – of the strategy, comparing these to the grammar of some basic Christian doctrines and looking at how they help us to recognise the Spirit.

## 1. INTRODUCTION: CROSSING THE BRIDGE

His aim [Henry Venn]... was the planting of indigenous churches. These were to be self-supporting, self-governing and self-extending. The missionary society was only the necessary scaffolding, the removal of which would leave the structure of the national church standing unassisted. So, well before colonial statesmen had devised a considered strategy of withdrawal towards self-determination in the British colonies and dependencies, Venn was carrying through a deliberate policy, based on the interim nature of the European and missionary presence, of bringing independent and indigenous churches into being. It is this policy which has caused the phrase 'the euthanasia of a mission' to be used, as Venn himself used it, to describe his central aim as a missionary statesman. Once the indigenous church was in being, the missionary society's work was done. The national church should be allowed to develop according to its own national character, with an indigenous leadership and episcopate, unstifled by the continuous presence of the European.

T. E. Yates[1]

Whenever I travel from home to Paddington on the train, I pass over Maidenhead Bridge. This viaduct is one of thoe marvels of Victorian engineering. Brunel's two arches are so flat that it was predicted the structure would collapse when the first train went over it. Local officials were so worried that they instructed Brunel to leave the scaffolding in place just in case the structure did collapse. During a gale the scaffolding was blown away and the bridge remained firm. 'The joke was that Brunel had been secretly aware of slight shrinkage or settlement in the [scaffolding] framework since the opening, and knew that it no longer supported the arches. Turner depicts this viaduct in his painting *Rain, Steam and Speed* hanging in the National Gallery.'[2]

The parallels between Yates' review of Venn's strategy for mission and Brunel's way of building bridges give us one way of understanding church mission societies. Within this perspective the mission society is the scaffolding, the means by which the structure of the church is built. When the church is complete, the scaffolding should be removed, be the church ever so unsteady. In fact it would be better if the scaffolding were blown away because people might not want to remove it. In all of this we may see the work of the Spirit: in the temporary scaffolding, the permanent structure and the gale!

This is an attractively clear approach to understanding how mission societies, committed to the church principle, should operate: endorsed by the Church, they are sent as the facilitating but temporary means by which the church is built elsewhere and then they move on. The aim is the establishing of a self-supporting, self-governing and self-extending church.

In this chapter I want to do two things: first, to reflect on the adequacy of this paradigm for church mission societies, and, secondly, to explore tentatively whether we are now moving into a new paradigm. In the first paradigm the Spirit is related to the scaffolding, structures and gale; in the paradigm that is emerging we could begin with the rain, steam and speed and then ask where we're going – it may be that our present context is much more that of a Turner than of a Venn or a Brunel!

## 2. FOUNDATIONS: A CHURCH MISSION SOCIETY

> I would sacrifice a great deal to preserve Church order, but not the salvation of souls.
>
> *John Venn*[3]

When it came to the doctrine of the Church, Venn may be seen as holding a kind of 'middle order' ecclesiology. The pietism of the eighteenth century had led to the rise of associations for the promotion of faith and holiness. This had its fruits on the continent, through Methodism in England and, not least, through the expression of the associational principle in the voluntary missionary societies founded in the 1790s. These associational bodies had shown themselves capable not only of supplementing but also of supplanting the institutional life of the churches within which they arose. Venn was heir both to the pietism that had given rise to the Evangelical revival and to the churchmanship that had led the founders of CMS to propose a 'church' society, which could combine the appeal and success of the earlier (and interdenominational) London Mission Society with what they regarded as the virtues of the ordered life, liturgy and ministry of the established Church . . . Bishops were seen certainly as of the plene esse of the church, as its chief pastors and leaders, but episcopacy was not fundamental to its being. Nevertheless, the office was to be respected for its antiquity and as expressive of godly government in the church according to the Anglican order; and on this understanding it was to be sought for the young churches where CMS was at work, who were incomplete without it.

*T. E. Yates*[4]

## Voluntary Associations in the Church

Once again we are indebted to Yates for a clear summary of Venn's approach. Here we have the foundational principles concerning the Church in relation to the mission society. It might be helpful to amplify a few points. First, the rise of associational bodies should not be seen purely as a religious matter. In the context of the English Church, religion was the civic and public means through which issues around new social patterns could emerge. To be a puritan was to have a different view on the polity of life as a whole and not just a difference of opinion on doctrinal matters or personal belief – belief, belonging, behaving and becoming were interlocked socially.

Secondly, it is worth noting that associational forms of Christianity have regularly emerged in the history of the Church. As Andrew Walls explains:

> The voluntary society, and its special form in the missionary society, arose in a particular period of Western social, political, and economic development and was shaped by that period. It was providentially used in God's purposes for the redemption of the world. But as Rufus Anderson noted long ago, it was but the modern, Western form of a movement that has periodically reappeared from an early period in Christian history. In one sense, monasteries were voluntary societies [and by them the gospel was spread] . . . From age to age it becomes necessary to use new means for the proclamation of the Gospel beyond the structures which unduly localise it. Some have taken the word 'sodality' beyond its special usage in Catholic practice to stand for all such 'use of means' by which voluntarily constituted groups labour together for specific gospel purposes. The voluntary societies have been as revolutionary in their

effect as ever the monasteries were in their sphere. The sodalities we now need may prove equally disturbing.

*A. Walls[5]*

The founders of CMS, who included John Venn, Henry's father, were committed to evangelistic mission[6] and also to the church principle. They proposed a mission society that would reflect both these commitments. Hennell writes, 'The question was could they do this "without being irregular" and "without infringing upon the order of the Establishment in any material point?"[7] The solution lay within the cultural context: the differentiated nature of English society and its internal pluralism had allowed for the emergence of associations. Such associations could make alliances (or not!) with institutional structures in pursuing matters of joint interest. The voluntary spirit, principle and organisation constitute a form of associational society, 'organs of initiative' as Max Warren called them. The Church Mission Society (as it's now called) sought endorsement, patronage and support from the establishment – from the Archbishop of Canterbury and leading bishops of the Church of England – for an association that would pursue world mission through an organisational structure running parallel to episcopal church governance. This was a 'mission out of order' and yet one endorsed by the existing order.

**For discussion:** *Is the voluntary association part of the Church or is it parachurch?*

## CMS and the established Church

For John Venn, the voluntary mission society was held in place in its relations with the wider Church by the establishment of the Church in society. The mission society could relate with a church 'by law established' on the basis of its own legal identity. In 1701 the Society for the Propagation of the Gospel had been granted a royal charter as a corporation in its own right; CMS sought to have its Society recognised as one that had a complementary ministry to SPG, being a Society committed to missionary outreach in Africa and Asia. It was Henry's father who proposed three principles for implementing this vision and a fourth for the pattern of governance:

- follow, do not anticipate God's leading;
- success will depend upon the kind of men employed;
- proceed from small beginnings

To these three fundamentals Venn added a fourth:

- the new Society should be 'founded upon the Church principle, not the High Church principle'.

Whereas on the one hand, Henry Venn rejected the LMS fundamental principle of evolving on the field 'such forms of Church Government as to the converts shall appear most agreeable to the Word of God', on the other hand, he realised that although the support of the bishops must be sought, they were neither going to be asked nor, if asked, were likely to accept the position they were given in the SPG. The new society was to be controlled by its own committee, not by bishops.

> The slowness with which CMS was recognised and supported might have had something to do with both the way in which the vision for outreach to Africa and Asia was implemented and with how the church principle was interpreted. The latter contrasted with the SPG's approach, which tended more to the 'chaplaincy' format. (There may also have been some questions in people's minds about the fledgling Society, given the fact that founding members of CMS were also promoting social change, for example, through an anti-slavery campaign.)

> The principles that Henry Venn inherited from his father required that he was constantly negotiating the policy of the Society in relation to the establishment. Unlike the SPG or the London Mission Society (LMS), CMS adopted a 'middle order' ecclesiology for how the mission society related to the established Church. This negotiated relationship was seen particularly in Venn's relations with bishops and with his view of episcopacy, which, for him, represented the Anglican order at its apex but was not of the essence of the Church.

It was not until the historic episcopate was affirmed as part of the principle of Anglicanism, in the Quadrilateral proposed by William Huntington, endorsed by the American bishops in 1886 and confirmed by Lambeth in 1888, that the Anglican order, which culminated in episcopacy, was affirmed outside the 'by law established' context of the Church of England. It was the non-established Protestant Episcopal Church of America that, reflecting on being deprived of episcopal ministry at one stage in its history and also drawing out an identity for Anglicanism from the ancient traditions of the Church, was driven to affirm the significance of the historic episcopate.

It is interesting to speculate on what Henry Venn would have made of the Quadrilateral and its influence on the Anglican Communion[8]. As it was, the work of CMS was overtaken by other developments, including the rise of the Keswick 'holiness movement', the Berlin agreement for the political division of Africa, and the appointment of a new leadership that was not committed to Venn's three-self strategy. These affected the response of CMS to the emerging Anglican Communion and probably affected its ability to make a strategic response to the Quadrilateral and its implications for world mission.

The tensions within Venn's negotiated 'middle order' began to show as the paradigm of 'territorial Christianity' slowly came under pressure. Venn relied on the Church-State relations of the established Church but, with the emergence of colonial contexts in which this pattern no longer operated (as illustrated by the Colenso affair), Venn's way of lobbying and relating to influential people could not work for long. One of the underdeveloped aspects of Venn's mission strategy was then exposed: the church principle did not include within its understanding of Church the means by which the gospel was spread, that is, the voluntary organisation. The next section deals with Venn's three-self strategy.

**For discussion:** *Can a church become para-mission without the presence of mission associations?*

## 2. GOAL: PLANTING THE THREE-SELF CHURCH

For practical purposes, the task of raising up indigenous churches to
be self-governing, self-supporting and self-propagating was almost
synonymous with the problem of raising up a native ministry.

*P.W. Harris*[9]

Venn's strategy for mission incorporates the notion of mission as scaffolding
and church as building. He deploys this imagery in developing the idea that
at the heart, the soul, of a mission there needs to be the establishing of a
'native church'. In other words, missionaries were to draw local converts into
the mission and were also to establish a native clergy, and, as such, they were
to see themselves as just builders of the local church: 'But as the building rises
the builders occupy less and less attention – the scaffolding becomes unsight-
ly and when the building is completed it is taken to pieces.'[10]

### Starting and building church

Thus, in Venn's mature thinking, 'Missionary work involved two tasks –
bringing people to Christ and the forming of a church[11]. The missionary was
essentially the evangelist and the native leaders would be increasingly the pastors within the newly-formed church.' For Venn this strategy was essential if
the mission was to press on to new parts and reach out to new regions. This
is only possible if the church that is planted is fully self-supporting, self-governing and self-extending, otherwise the mission will be employed in maintaining the church in one or more of these three dimensions. It is the euthanasia of a mission in the maintaining of the church in these dimensions that
Venn wishes to see; it is not the euthanasia of a mission itself so long as it still
has a vision for the regions beyond, for example, Paul's goal of getting to
Spain, having first built up the (three-self) church in Rome.

The tension in Venn's strategy is between the pattern of the established church
with the church principle as a foundation and that of the three-self church.
The euthanasia of a mission can never happen if the pattern of the Anglican
Church is used as the design for the three-self church: the problem is that the
mission plays a part that the order of Anglicanism does not include, that is,
the mission society itself, particularly in the capacity of evangelism. Thus the

mission society may not be expendable because the Anglican order will not make provision for the self-extension dimension of the church, either locally or in the taking of the gospel beyond the local region.

What the Anglican order does make provision for is the dimension of self-governance, particularly in the form of the historic episcopate. Venn was committed to self-governance, and in his vision of the planting of the local church one of his crowning achievements was the consecration of Samuel Crowther as Bishop on the Niger (1864-1890). The irony is that Crowther probably better represented the self-extension dimension of the church than the self-governing dimension.

> Venn hoped for the establishing of missionary churches but he did not make provision for this in revising the model of the church from which he was coming. Added to this was the difficulty of establishing the supplementary ministry of the mission association outside of the established church context. If the Church of England had not produced missionaries and evangelists except through the associational method, then how could the newly planted churches be any different if they followed the Anglican church order? It is questionable whether missionary churches, dioceses or congregations can ever exist; it may be that such work is always the provenance of those with a calling and ability for such work. What a church can do to enable itself to have such a dimension is to include the agency for apostolic mission as part of the principle of its self-understanding.

**For discussion**: *Can truly missionary churches, dioceses or congregations ever exist?*

### The promise and challenge of Uganda

The Tucker period in Uganda (1890-1911) offered one opportunity when an alternative model could have been developed. At the beginning of the last century a situation arose in Uganda whereby the missionaries wanted to remain outside the control of the local church, and the local church, under a missionary bishop (Tucker), wanted them to be more accountable, more integrated.

CMS was caught between encouraging accountability and losing control. The missionaries were, eventually, placed outside the constitution of the Church of Uganda – their affairs were dealt with by a separate board. Inadvertently, they were, therefore, repeating the associational relation by accident – they were outside the established Church! However, they were neither sponsored nor supported by the local church. The key issue here was the question of governance: were the missionaries to be placed under the local church or not? The missionaries argued for retaining their independence but probably for the wrong reason.

> The voluntary structure of self-extension was not replicated in the Uganda context, so the status of the missionaries was raised under the dimension of self-governance, where it became a question of power. However, if CMS does not look too good in all this, then at least, as Williams concludes, 'If it has been established that the Society was cautious and compromising and anxious to preserve its own power, it has not been proved that it was motivated by racialism in its reluctance to support Tucker in working through his principles of integration.'[12] (op cit: p. 255)

> As it was, an alternative missionary movement did emerge. 'In many parts of Africa, expatriate missionaries depended heavily on African catechists, but probably in few areas was there an indigenous expansion of Christianity comparable to that in Uganda between 1890 and 1914.'[13] Uganda was evangelised primarily by the Ugandans and not by the Europeans and this was done by catechists who were locally commissioned and paid. The sad thing is that there was a failure to integrate and develop African leadership that would maintain this movement as part of the order of the Church in Uganda. The result was that the vitality of the Ugandan Church declined and reached a low ebb between the wars. Pirouet concludes of this period, 'The goal of a self-supporting, self-governing, and self-propagating church was largely abandoned in fact if not in theory, and white missionaries seemed to consider themselves a permanently necessary scaffolding.'[14] The three-self policy works if the self-extending dimension is planted as a self-supporting

and self-governing dimension of the church that is planted. Where this does not happen and is not consciously included in the church, then alternative forms of self-propagation may emerge but may never be fully integrated.

## The church principle and bishops

The 'church principle' is an important one because it forces this kind of think-ing to be incorporated into mission strategy. It is worth noting that, from the more Catholic perspective, the missionary bishop represented the incorpora-tion into church order of both the affirmation of the church, with its focus in the bishop, and the importance of the agency for mission. Venn did not find this strategy acceptable. He disliked the deployment of missionary bishops, not just because he struggled with Tractarian theology but because it went against his views about how the local church should be built. In Venn's view, the native bishop is the crown of the structure, the apex of the building. If, however, missionary bishops are brought in from the beginning, a truly indigenous leadership will not be encouraged, but rather the pattern of church which the bishop brings will be a transplant that will only lead to dependency on a foreign agency and pattern of church.

> This does not mean that Venn did not support the appointment of some missionaries who became bishops. In fact at the consecration of one of them he preached about the importance of the bishop in mission, using the example of the church at Antioch. The bishop is not essential to mis-sion but he can, and should, do mission. 'Venn argued that the Antioch experience did not demonstrate that a bishop was the mainstay of a mis-sion. The personal qualifications of the man rather than the office deter-mined his effectiveness. The bishop must evidence the fruits of the Spirit. He sustained others by his example and faith.' Again, 'A bishop proved his missionary leadership by his own spirituality, by promoting spiritual growth in his people, and by encouraging those specially com-missioned for missionary work.'[15] Crowther was to have been an exam-ple of this kind of bishop: 'Venn's ideal for Crowther foundered on the determined opposition of the European missionaries and the past histo-ry of criticism and bitterness over Crowther's family . . . To have made

Crowther Bishop of Lagos over the established Yoruba mission with a developing Lagos Native Pastorate in African hands, with an indigenous church self-governing and self-supporting in view, and self-propagating in the Niger Mission, the whole enterprise overseen by an African bishop, would have combined all Venn's aims.'[16] As it was, Crowther was responsible for the Niger only, and the Yoruba region was never transferred to his jurisdiction.

**For discussion:** *In what ways does Anglican church order encourage or restrict the development of mission?*

### 4. CONTEXT: THE EMERGENCE OF WORLD CHURCH

The missionary movement is in some respects the last flourish of the Christendom idea.

A. Walls [17]

'In terms of total Christian history the missionary movement may prove to be the single most important development in modern Western Christianity.'[18] This is the judgement of Andrew Walls, a distinguished and influential historian of mission. Walls' evaluation, however, is not reflected in the way that the Anglican Church is sometimes introduced. The modern missionary movement, to which Anglicans have made a significant contribution and out of which sprang many of the member churches of the Anglican Communion, is often treated as peripheral to Anglican identity: it simply doesn't fit into Anglican church order, yet it has profound implications for Anglican identity.

**The last flourish of Christendom!**
For Walls, the origins of the missionary movement were 'in the territorial idea of Christianity, the association of the faith with one part of the world, the "fully missionized lands" of 1910, from which the word may go forth to the "not yet fully missionized lands" elsewhere.'[19] Yet as Walls goes on to say, the mission movement is also the greatest challenge to the Christendom idea in the way that it has encouraged the break-up of Christendom thinking: 'The territorial "from-to" idea that underlay the older missionary movement has to give way to a concept much more like that of Christians within the Roman

Empire in the second and third centuries: parallel presences in different circles and at different levels, each seeking to penetrate within and beyond its circle.' Thus the emergence of the Western missionary movement is significant not only for the outcome, that is, that the gospel was spread around the world, but also for the break-up of Christendom, of territorial Christianity. Walls' argument may be summarised in three theses:

1. Western Christianity has taken the form of Christendom, 'a conception in which Christianity was essentially linked to territory and the possession of territory';
2. one of the major solvents of Christendom was colonialism;
3. the serial expansion of Christianity through the missionary movement meant that Christianity was diffused in a non-Christendom manner; it was not Christendom-bound.

Walls suggests that Christian expansion is serial – an expansion that takes place at the periphery. A most significant peripheral expansion of Christianity was among the northern and western barbarians at the edge of the Roman Empire, a form of territorial Christianity in which conversion was not of the individual but of the tribal nation: the symbolic reordering of a community with a single body of custom.

> This could never have happened within Constantine's empire, which 'had too much diversity, too many interest groups, too much inbuilt pluralism'. However, the combination of territory with the universalising tendencies of the Roman Empire produced Christendom, whereby territories were related to a wider territory in which there was 'a single civilization of fused elements from the Celtic and Germanic cultures with what it could absorb from the Roman Empire, and preserved that Empire's language for the purpose of learning, worship and wider communication after it had ceased to be anyone's vernacular.' The Hellenistic contribution to Christianity was the idea of orthodoxy, the 'barbarian' contribution was territorialism, leading to 'a state ruled according to Christian norms expressed through a single recognized channel.'[20]

The modern missionary movement has sprung from this heritage and yet has also been responsible for undermining it. The work of the voluntary societies as a missionary movement outside the official aspects of colonialism, as Walls goes on to write:

> Gradually introduced a principle of separation between the religion of Christendom and its political, military and economic power. Colonialism, in fact, helped to transform the Christian position in the world by forcing a distinction between Christianity and Christendom. Colonial experience undermined the identification of Christianity and territory and immobilized the idea of crusade. The missionary period may have once been associated with the colonial powers but it is also true to say that during the same period there was a separation between religion and Western powers. Paradoxically, and in sharp contrast to its first vision, colonialism helped to ensure that new Christendoms did not arise.[21]

## Grappling with territorial Christianity

The separation between Christianity and territory was one that did not come easily in the development of Anglican world mission. The fact that episcopacy, as part of the principle for the order of the Church, ties the Church into a territorial Christianity is one aspect – a bishop is nearly always a bishop of somewhere. However, the diocesan and parish model for ordering the church system is just one model and, as we know from the history of the Church in Britain, there was another way of being church and another way of interpreting the place of episcopacy, that is, the Celtic Church. Thus the historic episcopacy of the Quadrilateral may imply one model for historic episcopacy that presumes the territorial and established background that slowly emerged in the English context, but the Celtic context and that of the third millennium are different. The Celtic model of episcopacy is one set in the context of the wider vision of apostolic, evangelistic mission. Here faith and order is related to the principle of a church committed to evangelistic mission.[22]

In today's world we are in a non-establishment, cultural context in which our mission aim is not to win a re-establishment but to do evangelistic mission in a pluralistic, postmodern context. We need some kind of radical orthodoxy that will release us anew into the agency for apostolic mission, the order of becoming an evangelistic world Church. We have been held captive by a picture and it's time to find a new 'mission out of order'! Let's look at what happened when the old order was stretched by CMS's support for a new Bishop (G. Smith), based in Hong Kong, whose 'territory' had been expanded by the Crown (in 1849) to include all of China.

> CMS came under criticism on the grounds that, by introducing the jurisdiction of the bishop of Hong Kong into Shanghai they were contravening the ancient practice of the church, that only one bishop should work in one place, as laid down at the Council of Nicea.
>
> T. E. Yates[23]

The complaint was that CMS had supported and recognised the episcopal governance of the Bishop of Victoria over an area that the American Episcopal Church had included in its episcopal region of Shanghai. The response made by CMS (that is, the Committee [influenced by Venn]) was that '"the committee cannot recognise any other jurisdiction, in any part of the world, than that of the episcopate of the United Church of England and Ireland, under the authority of Her Majesty by her Letters Patent and of the Archbishop of Canterbury".'[24]

The fascinating thing here is that what is at issue is the nature of the Church, particularly its territorial nature. Drawing on the precedent of the ancient Church, the Americans were complaining about the lack of territorial sensitivity of the British Church, despite the fact that they had set up parallel jurisdictions in Turkey and Jerusalem. CMS responded that it only recognised certain territorial claims in any part of the world, and that the ancient Church offered examples of parallel territorial jurisdiction anyway. What was more, it asserted that the territorial notions of the American Church, with its voluntary association of parishes to form a diocese, was alien to the English model. The irony was, of course, that this was the response of a voluntary association! All this only illustrates a fundamental point: mission was stretching the inherited models of Anglicanism – whether the established pattern of the Church of England or the reconstructed pattern of the Protestant Episcopal Church of America – which looked to the ancient roots of the Church (and that was eventually to lead to the development of the Anglican Quadrilateral, which both the American and the gathered, largely English, bishops at the Lambeth Conference were to accept).

**For discussion:** *Are Anglicans held captive by the picture of a territorial Christianity in their church order?*

## 5. CONSTRUCTIVE REFLECTIONS: THE CMS HERITAGE FOR TODAY'S 'MISSIOLOGIC'[25]

When I refer to Spirit Christology, I do so in an orthodox way that preserves the trinitarian distinctions. Spirit Christology enriches but does not replace Logos Christology. It enriches Logos Christology by doing great justice to the role of the Spirit in Christ. It gives better recognition to the missions of both the Son and the Spirit. It neither exaggerates nor diminishes the role of either Person. I am indebted to Eastern Orthodox theology, which has always maintained that Western traditions have diminished the role of the Spirit by giving the Son an ontic and the Spirit a noetic role.[26]

Reflecting on what we have appreciated from the CMS mission-strategy legacy, what can we say about recognising the movement of the Spirit in mission? Let me suggest that one way of doing this is to move beyond the images of scaffolding and structure: to acknowledge that this is one pattern for the faith and order of the church principle - the grammar of mission strategy. Within the strategy we have reviewed we have reversed Anglican development: we have moved from system (by law established) to principle (three-self) to provisional church order (territorial Christianity). This is not comfortable but it may be where we are being led as we are drawn out in response to the Spirit to develop a new mission strategy for an emerging new world order. The pattern for the future is not clear and it may be that we will continue to move in a divergent rather than convergent manner: towards an open church strategy

– a fellowship or 'community of the Spirit'.[27] This does not mean that we will end in chaos, but we may find ourselves in 'chaorder'. Recognising patterns of the work of the Spirit may be one way in which we will be able to discern if it is God at work.

> In what follows I review three patterns of the grammar of mission strategy (missio-logic) by relating mission to some basic grammar of faith (traditional and emerging): Chalcedonian Christology, Trinitarian relations and emerging Spirit-Christology. I shall be reflecting primarily on the patterns of the implied relations for mission and also considering what has been emphasised and what could be re-emphasised. My basic point is that the Spirit is seen in these patterns of relations and that these patterns are the grammar of a mission strategy committed to a church principle.

### From scaffolding and structure to complementary ministries

Henry Venn's understanding of mission in relation to proclaiming the gospel and establishing churches contained an inherent contradiction. The churches that CMS established did not organise themselves structurally around the priority of evangelistic mission because they replicated the order of the Anglican Church, but did not organise the church around the principle of the three-self church. In Church-of-England Anglicanism, where self-governance is emphasised and incorporates self-support, the structure of self-extension is missing. In this Anglicanism, self-extension is done by voluntary societies and these are not seen as part of the structure unless they are drawn into, or are a product of, a mission board linked with synodical/episcopal governance. Even here, however, the notion of governance is probably dominated by territorial Christianity. We probably need a new order. The cultural disestablishment of the Church from modernity and the alienation of people from the institutional Church has brought this home and taught us hard lessons in evangelism.

Put simply in three points, this new order might be as follows:

1. the Church as a whole is seen as a voluntary mission society;
2. there are two main operational ministries for enabling this to happen: mission as pastoral ministry and mission as evangelism ministry;

3. these two ministries both share in the governance of the voluntary mission and management of ministry through a collegial mutuality.

One way of exploring the grammar of this proposal would be to draw out the potential missiologic of Chalcedon: transposing 'not dividing the substance nor confounding the persons' into not dividing the mission nor confounding the ministries. The Spirit brings us one mission and in that one mission there is a dipolarality of mission ministry. The pattern of this missiologic would allow for a mutuality between self-support (formerly thought of as structure and maintenance) and self-extension (formerly scaffolding and mission). In this missiologic we would not call one ministry or dimension 'the Church' and the other 'para-church' (or even 'para-mission'). Rather we would recognise that the Church is fundamentally a mission movement that is more than the ministry, and that single identity cannot be thought to reside substantially in either of the polarities of expressing that mission but only in the Church as a whole. Church governance may be seen to symbolise the unity of the mission ministry in so far as it is the collegial mutuality of ministry, but the mission identity of the Church is not thereby confined to the governance of ministry. One way of reworking this would be to talk about priestly (support), prophetic (extension) and kingly mission (governance). All these, however, are part of the fundamental reality of Christian witnesses (movement), the Spirit's wisdom.

> This has major implications for Anglican identity and Anglican church order where church support (pastoral) and church governance (episcopacy) have incorporated the wider witness of Christians through shared ministry and synodical governance. We do not seem, however, to have been able to integrate church extension into a broader pattern. I doubt that this produces a church which has a fundamental mission identity (substance) and the rise of the voluntary societies indicate that this pattern has not worked – they constitute a division of the mission substance of the Church that emerged within the context of territorial Christianity. My sense is that we have modified territorial Christianity but we have not yet incorporated the radical implications of the voluntary associations.

**For discussion:** *Has Anglican order confounded the ministries and thereby divided the substance of mission?*

### From three-self church to self-othering mission

The second theme relates to the nature of the mission of self-supporting, self-governing and self-extending churches. The issue here is that the three-self church is not necessarily a church that is reciprocal in its mission relations. There can be, and has been, a linear pattern in such relations which is a one-way paradigm in the Christendom 'from-to' style. We have now to accept that this is inappropriate. CMS has talked first of 'partnership' and then 'interchange' as being key ways of understanding mission relations. Here I want to draw out this missiologic as a Trinitarian one.

> The aim of mission societies has been so to move out of one's own culture and move into another's that it is the extension of the church of the gospel and not the extension of the self that is planted. One of the great criticisms of the missionary movement was that it failed to do this. Venn himself suggested that the aim was not to Anglicise others but to bring the gospel only. Of course this was difficult to do, though in the translation of the Scriptures into various mother tongues we see a commitment to try to do this, which has had a huge impact. The tricky thing is that territorial expansion and self-extension are closely allied within modern Christendom. Indeed, the 'self' is so important to the Enlightenment period that the use of the word betrays the fact that the missionary movement was a product of Venn's time. How do we find an alternative way of expressing this pattern of mission?

> One way is to explore J. V. Taylor's use of the term 'in-othering' as an expression of Trinitarian co-inherence (perichoresis). For Taylor, in-othering is a mutual indwelling of another. This kind of indwelling of another is one that John Taylor has associated with the Holy Spirit. Taylor has suggested that the 'Go-Between God' is the God who creates the community of mutual indwelling. This is the fellowship into which Christians are invited to share through prayer. In mission, the greater self of God in his in-othering of us is the basis and model for the evan-

gelistic mission of the Church. In God's mission there is not an expansion by territorial self-extension but a self-othering, in which there is kenosis and mutual enriching (plenosis), that images the mutual enrichment of the Trinity. Thus, for Taylor, in-othering is a supernatural and natural truth: 'It is the nature of things because it is the nature of God as Trinity, as Love: the Self-Giver, the Self-Given and the in-othered Spirit. Since this is the mystery of God's own being it has been also the means whereby God saves the world.' In summary, 'God's love for the world is an overflow of the eternal exchange within the Trinity.'[28]

If we were to modify the three-self understanding of the Church we might therefore want to talk about a self-othering church: a church that is willing to give itself away and be enriched by another in the sharing of the gospel. Otherwise, a three-self church can simply duplicate itself rather than truly engage with an other. In-built into the three-self model there must be a willingness to lose self and gain self. The willingness for sacrificial self-extension through self-othering is a sign that the self is not the focus but rather it is God who is self-othering in relation to both himself and to the world. The self-othering of mission is analogous to the relations of the Trinity, in which self-extension can be understood as a going beyond into new regions of relational depth in which the presence of God will be found transcendent in the midst. We catch a glimpse of this in one of those purple passages from Taylor's The Primal Vision:

> ...areas of need are not, surely, the limit of his Realm. His is no carrion-comfort feeding on dissolution; and his presence with Man is not only at the place of his defeat but also at the place of his vision, to preserve and fulfil whatever in it has been true and strong. It is the lordship of Christ which is in question. Either he is the Lord of all possible worlds and all human cultures, or he is Lord of one world and one culture only. Either we must think of the Christian Mission in terms of bringing the Muslim, the Hindu, the Animist into Christendom, or we must go with Christ as he stands in the midst of Islam, of Hinduism, of the primal world-view, and watch with him, fearfully and wonderingly, as he becomes – dare we say it

– Muslim or Hindu or Animist, as once he became Man, and a Jew. Once, led by the Spirit, the Church made its choice in this matter at the Council of Jerusalem and dared to win Gentiles by becoming Gentile. Paul and those who followed him did not wait for history to reduce the Graeco-Roman world to chaos and drive its derelicts into the arms of the Church. They claimed that world in its strength and reformulated the Gospel in the terms of its wisdom. So Christ in his Church answered the call of the Greeks; he came where they were and became what they were. From within their own culture he challenged their strength and judged their wisdom. He turned their world upside down, just as he had turned Judaism upside down – just as, indeed, he enters our Churches today and he turns our Christianity upside down. So would he challenge and judge and revolutionize the African world-view; but he must do it from the inside.[29]

With this vision we are drawn deeper into prayer and into new understandings of faith.

The practical outworking would be an everyday mission spirituality also expressed in the various dimensions of the three-self church as re-ordered in the last section. At this level we are talking about the imagination of and for mission, in which the self of the three-self church is expanded by a self-othering mission, the mission of the greater self of the three-personed in-othering God.

**For discussion:** *What stirs up our prayer life and our imagination, drawing us into a new mission spirituality?*

### 'Rain, steam and speed': towards a Spirit movement

The new world order, which is emerging, will bring the final end to Christendom. The grammar of the mission strategy into which we are being called is still emerging. However, I would suggest that in addition to our Chalcedonian and Trinitarian patterns we may see the emergence of another: the grammar of Spirit-Christology. Spirit-Christology can include traditional Christological and Trinitarian perspectives. It can be approached systematically and/or through key images that imply the logical relations. For me, the term *paraclesis* (to comfort and to challenge) has become a significant way of focusing what I am seeking in terms of resourcing and envisioning a mission spirituality that can move beyond territorial Christianity. The concentricity and organisational character of the inherited modes and patterns of church are giving way to emerging, new patterns of church.

The challenge for contemporary mission is the future culture and not just cross-cultural outreach. We are in a situation in which our background culture is disappearing and a new world order, which is both local and global, is emerging. We need a way of finding God in all this and a way of relating the God we find to the God we have already known. We also need, however, a transitional strategy (hopefully, not an exit strategy) that will both carry us forward and be the harbinger of things to come. Such confidence can only be born of knowing the One who can encourage us.

**Foundations for future mission**

The following theological reflections are from CMS' planning document, exploring the theological foundations for the mission in the forthcoming years.

Recent theology has highlighted the difference between procession and return (or reciprocity) models of the Trinity. Both models have been influenced by the twentieth-century axiom that the way God relates to himself as Trinity is seen in the way God relates to the world. This idea may be formulated as follows: 'the immanent Trinity is the same as the economic Trinity', that is, God's 'internal' relation to himself is the same as God's relation to himself as revealed in mission. This is an important idea for the foundation of mission. This axiom is significant for CMS because the Society's present stage of development coincides with the strengthening of reciprocity models of the Trinity. In Spirit-Christology the Spirit is understood as the personification and enabling of the Father-Son relationship as this is revealed in the coming and returning of the Son to the Father in mission. The Church is called and caught up into this mission, in which all things are being drawn up by the Spirit in a return to God the Father.

The terms *paraclete* and *paraclesis* help us to explore a Spirit-Christological perspective on the character of God and his mission. St John's Gospel portrays Jesus as the first, and the Spirit as the second, Paraclete – the one who is co-present alongside us (John 14:16). In Paul, God's co-presence is known in *paraclesis* – an encouragement that is both challenging and comforting. A missiology founded on Spirit-Christology is a missiology of God's encouraging co-presence at the heart of created human existence. This is enacted in the incarnation of God in Jesus' life, the life he offered in obedient sacrifice (supremely on the cross), comforting (being with) us in our sin and suffering, and yet also challenging us to a new life of holiness and discipleship. God's mission as Paraclete is revealed in this *paraclesis*: he is the God of all encouragement (2 Corinthians 1:8). God's greatest encouragement for new life is the Resurrection, continued in God's ongoing redemption of the world – the long resurrection. The Holy Spirit draws all creation into the long resurrection and encourages the building up of the Church's mission, growth in church numbers and a maturing in mission spirituality (Acts 9:31).

The calling to be part of God's long resurrection is an eschatological (the ultimate goal of all things) calling, which requires that we plan for the future (the penultimate). The link between the return model of God's Trinitarian mission and eschatology invites an appropriation of future studies (the exploration of trends in human society). Tomorrow's world challenges us to think about tomorrow's mission and tomorrow's Church. It is not primarily that mission organisations need to predict and prepare for future change, but rather that mission is fundamentally about God's plan for our future in Christ – 'a plan for the fullness of time, to gather up all things in him' (Ephesians 1:10 NRSV). Sensitivity to how this plan relates to what is, and to what may happen, in the world can be helped by future studies. They are currently suggesting that institutional forms of Church (but not belief) in the West are collapsing under the processes of globalisation!

The missiologic of Spirit-Christology is that God has opened himself up to creation to be involved in an ongoing way. This is expressed in the

Incarnation, is an overflow of the life of the Trinity and has the character of encouragement as this is seen in the past and present work of the Spirit. The Spirit maintains the openness of God to the world and of the world to God in an engagement in which the future is still emerging. God's vulnerability in this engagement is measured by the depth of his encouragement. The Spirit's presence in the world is in the rain, steam and speed of the ongoing change in which we are all caught up. Emerging church initiatives are rediscovering the church principle in a new way that reflects this kind of Presence: they are exploring how they link with the inherited Church and they are reworking the three-self principle, but they also want to connect all this with what is happening in the world around them.

CMS is repositioning itself in relation to what the Spirit seems to be saying. The aim is to discern a way forward that incorporates the most radical guidance by the Spirit but encourages the transition across from one side to the other.[30]

The recently produced CMS report Filling the Gaps by D. Strange is subtitled 'Church Planting/New Ways of Being Church in a Post-Christian Britain'. This says something about where we are now and where we once started. We want to learn how to go forward with a God who is open to us and to the future, and is encouraging us to step out again with the gospel. It's a bit chaotic but we trust in the God of the long resurrection who encourages us into new life with the encouragement that passes through death.

What kind of shape does this Turneresque picture give the Church? Let me leave you with some words from the last report of Missio (a committee of the Anglican Consultative Council). Having acknowledged the mix of structures within Anglicanism, that is, parishes, dioceses, orders and societies, the authors go on to say:

> A theological framework for this mix of structures for worship, service and witness is to see the Church as a movement, the pilgrim people of God journeying to the Kingdom. Within this large movement,

there arise many smaller movements as faithful Christians seek, under the Spirit, to fulfil their vocations in a variety of ways. Such movements may be about evangelisation, issues of justice and peace, and advocacy for the powerless.[31]

I believe that Spirit-Christology can provide us with the missiologic for such a mission movement, a movement in which there is a plurality and richness of mission relations.

**For discussion:** *What practical difference does theology make to mission strategy or mission strategy to theology?*

### Notes

[1] T. E. Yates, *Venn and Victorian Bishops Abroad*, SPCK, 1978, p. 16f., (my italics).

[2] J. M. and S. Pearce, *Twyford and the Great Western Railway*, Twyford and Ruscombe Local History Society, 1994, p. 9f.

[3] M. Hennell, *John Venn and the Clapham Sect*, Lutterworth Press, 1958, p.234.

[4] T. E. Yates, op. cit., p. 195.

[5] A Walls, 'Missionary Societies and the Fortunate Subverion of the Church' in, *The Missionary Movement in Christian History*, T & T Clark, 1996, p.252f.

[6] The first Law of the Society is: 'The Church Mission Society (CMS) is a voluntary association of people united in obedience to the call of God to proclaim the Gospel in all lands and to gather the people of all races into the fellowship of Christ's Church.' (Revised version, 1995)

[7] M. Hennell, op. cit., p. 232.

[8] Yates tells us that Venn was 'wary of the American church and is missions', op. cit., p. 91f.; see also n. 57 loc. cit.

[9] P. W. Harris, *Nothing But Christ: Rufus Anderson and the Ideology of Protestant Foreign Missions*, OUP, 1999, p. 113.

[10] Henry Venn's correspondence, 1860.

[11] P. Williams, op. cit., p. 157.

[12] P. Williams, op. cit., p. 255.

[13] L. Pirouet, *Black Evangelists: The Spread of Christianity in Uganda 1891-1914*, Rex Collins, 1978, p. 195.

[14] L. Pirouet, op. cit., p. 193.

[15] W. R. Shenk, *Henry Venn—Missionary Statesman*, Orbis, 1983, p.29.

[16] T. E. Yates, op. cit., p. 157.

[17] A. Walls, 'The Old Age of the Missionary Movement', op. cit., p. 258.

[18] A. Walls, 'Christianity in the non-western world: a study in the serial nature of Christian expansion', in James P. Mackey (ed.), *Studies in World Christianity*, Edinburgh University Press, 1995, p. 9.

[19] A. Walls, 'The Old Age of the Missionary Movement', op. cit., p. 258.

[20] A. Walls, 'The Old Age of the Missionary Movement', op. cit., pp. 11, 12, 13.

[21] A. Walls, 'The Old Age of the Missionary Movement', op. cit., p. 21.

[22] For a non-idealised account of the Celtic mission, see J. Finney, *Recovering the Past*, DLT, 1996

[23] T. E. Yates, op. cit., p. 90.

[24] ibid.

[25] This is the title for All Nations Christian College's occasional papers on mission—I wish I'd thought of it first!

[26] C. Pinnock, *Flame of Love*, IVP, 2000, p. 92.

[27] See L. Newbigin's classic text, *The Household of God*, SCM, 1957, ch. 4.

[28] J. V. Taylor, *The Christlike God*, SCM, 1992, pp. 250, 251.

[29] J. V. Taylor, *The Primal Vision*, SCM, 1963, p. 113 (my emphasis).

[30] J. Finney's, *Fading Splendour*, DLT, 2000, is an example of an understanding of renewal for transitional church.

[31] E. Johnson and J. Clark (eds), SPCK, 2000, p. 63.

# 6. An experiment in Christian community

## TONY HODGSON

When looking at our aspirations for community, does the practice of a counter-culture actually have any impact on the status quo? What can we learn from the experience of living in a Christian community?

*Tony Hodgson spent twenty-five years in rural ministry and four years at Christ Church, Lancaster Gate, London. He refounded the Little Gidding Community. Little Gidding is a powerful symbol for some in the Church of England today. It speaks of a way of being church that is neither rigidly monastic nor part of the parish system, yet authentically biblical, providing a haven of peace and a place for spiritual renewal. Here Tony shares his experience.*

My main experience of living in community took place some twenty-five years ago in a tiny hamlet in Huntingdonshire called Little Gidding and my involvement in that community lasted just four years. Those four years, however, left a lasting impression on my thinking, so that ever since I have tended to judge the parishes which I have served in the light of the community in which I lived.

### HOSPITALITY

At Little Gidding one of our main purposes was to provide hospitality to the many visitors who passed that way. We were open to people of all ages, backgrounds, races and spiritual outlooks to join us for ten minutes, two weeks or six months. And they did. We had a particular magnetism for the young, the dispossessed, the seekers. The constant flow of visitors stopped us becoming an inward-looking clique and helped us to earth our ideas in the everyday lives of people living in the world.

## SIMPLICITY

One of the things that young people find attractive in a community is the willingness to let go both of the past and of present possessions. Taizé have a rule that they call the power of the provisional. This includes throwing away all past records since those who join the community wish to live in a way that is uncluttered. At Little Gidding some of our visitors were kind enough to relieve us of some of our surplus possessions!

## SHARING

Community is about sharing, not only of individual possessions, important as those are, but of our whole selves. The sharing of meals, of work, of prayer and of celebration on a daily, not an occasional basis, meant that we became deeply involved in each other's lives.

## ACCEPTANCE

Such differences as denominations or churchmanship were largely irrelevant – few young people were or are the slightest bit concerned about the battles of the past that have created the divisions of the present. We therefore made space for different approaches to God to coexist side by side, by, for instance, alternating formal and informal prayer.

Mixing with people from different social or racial backgrounds once a week on a Sunday is different from having to eat and work with them day by day. Their different table manners, their different ways of bringing up children, even their different ways of saying words may grate unless one learns to become profoundly accepting.

The key to the success of any community is the involvement of all who belong to it. The young played an important part in the life of the community, but so did the old and the middle-aged. No one was crowded out. All decision-making depended on the agreement of all who belonged, and the voiceless were listened to as much as the vocal.

## BALANCE

There was a good balance between the importance of work with the hands and work with the head. The community depended for a large part of its food on those who grew the vegetables, milked the cows and made the butter. These skills were valued just as highly as the skills of those who led the worship – and, of course, the same people did both.

Communities can be places of immense creativity, and those who joined the community found they had scope to develop hidden gifts, whether in music, arts, gardening, building, crafts, dance or any other expression.

## COMMITMENT

All communities demand a high level of commitment and all members were invited to review that commitment on a regular basis. There could be no passengers since, if someone was not contributing to the life of the community as well as drawing from it, there was little point in being involved.

## 'SMALL IS BEAUTIFUL'

Numbers are of little significance. The very nature of Little Gidding made it impossible to become large and we rejoiced in that, as long as our smallness did not denote any suggestion of being a closed shop.

One of the reasons why we did not mind being small was that our three main foci were a tiny chapel, a home and a small piece of land. If one has a large building to fill, it can be a constant worry, and one of the joys of Little Gidding church was that if there were six people there it was full and if there were thirty it was overflowing.

Our small piece of land, eight acres in all, from which we provided half the food for an average of twenty people, also conveyed a message that food does not have to be produced in larger and larger units.

## CARE FOR THE ENVIRONMENT

Each community needs to have at least one particular concern beyond the community itself. At Little Gidding one of our main thrusts was to develop a way of living on the land that was gentle with soil, with plants, with animals and with all the material things that God has given us. In common with other communities, we found that this concentration on an object beyond ourselves meant that our way of life was seen as profoundly relevant by many for whom church was no longer a significant part of their lives.

## STILLNESS

Situated as we were in a secluded spot of considerable beauty, we offered people a place of peace. The desire for stillness, for quiet reflection and to learn ways of meditation is widespread in our society, and communities can respond to this need.

The Little Gidding Community was first founded in the turbulent seventeenth century by Nicholas Ferrar, and lasted for about thirty years. When he handed over the leadership to his brother, he said, 'It is the right, good, old way you are in; keep in it.' Communities like Little Gidding are prophetic voices to the Church today.

# 7. The example of basic ecclesial communities

## JOHN SUMMERS

In moving towards new models of being church, how do we avoid our natural propensity to institutionalise the process?

If not granted by standard Anglican authority, through what agents are we able to recognise the grass roots' will to change?

*John Summers became Vicar of St Barnabas Church, Plymouth, in 1981 and is now retired. He is active in the* New Way of Being Church *network, and has derived great inspiration from the experience of basic ecclesial communities in Latin America. Here he describes how his church in Plymouth applied some of the principles of these communities and became more outward-looking.*

> I believe that the worldwide emergence of Basic Ecclesial Communities is the work of the Holy Spirit in our time, a gift of God to the Church. For this reason they have a central place in our diocesan vision and I encourage parishes to move towards them as a long-term orientation and 'preferred way' for our local church.
>
> *Leonard Faulkner – Roman Catholic Archbishop of Adelaide*

Over recent years I have come across more and more people who are disillusioned with the Church. These people are not anti-Christian. Often they have a firm commitment to Christ and his gospel. But they find it increasingly difficult to cope with the Church and the way it operates. What I propose to do here is to tell our story, then to offer a brief reflection on the experience, and finally to suggest possible courses of action. This is to follow a process that is fundamental to those of us who are involved in developing a New Way of Being Church. Known as the 'pastoral cycle', this process has three stages:

1. see
2. reflect
3. act

# 1. SEE

### The story of an Anglican parish

I became vicar of the inner-urban parish of St Barnabas, Plymouth, in 1981 after a vacancy of two years and found a rather dispirited, middle-of-the-road Anglican church with a small, mainly elderly, congregation. Over the next few years, the church was led in an evangelical and gently charismatic direction and developed into a lively local community church. The church had a strong sense of being a family, and its worship was characterised by flexibility and informality. The local culture was mixed, but mainly working-class, and most of those who participated in the life of the church lived locally.

Over the years we tried unsuccessfully to redevelop the very large Victorian church building into something more appropriate for present-day needs. Progress was depressingly slow and the long delay sapped the enthusiasm and energy of many.

One key member of the church, however, urged us to use the resources we already had (despite the shortcomings of the existing building) and to work as much as possible with the local community. We realised that the church was the only building large enough to be a meeting-place for local people, so we decided to open it up for community use in order to provide a venue for public meetings dealing with local issues. So began the Barnabas Community Project. This was the stage we had reached in 1994.

#### Introduction to Liberation Theology

It was during 1993 that I became aware of the theology of Latin America and began to read Liberation theologians such as Boff, Sobrino, Gustavo Gutierrez and others. I came to it with the common perception that this new theology was a dangerous form of Marxism that threatened to subvert Christianity, but what I actually found was the radical application of the gospel to everyday life. It was good news for today, especially for the poor, the oppressed and those who were on the margins of society.

The Bible was central, but it was used in a way that was new and disconcerting. Yet this approach seemed right and it made the word of God accessible and relevant to ordinary theologically untrained people. I devoured this 'new' material and was intrigued and excited by it. The approach was very different from anything I had met before and at first I found it hard to get used to a new way of thinking. However, my conviction grew that here was something important and relevant for us in Britain.

### The 'Marins' New Way of Being Church workshops

It all began to come together in 1994 when I took part in a New Way of Being Church workshop led by a Brazilian Roman Catholic priest, Jose Marins, who, as a member of the theological reflection team to CELAM (the Latin and Caribbean Catholic Bishops Conference), has for over thirty years been a facilitator to the basic ecclesial communities (BECs) throughout Latin America.

The workshop was very different from any in which I had participated before and it proved to be the most significant and radical turning-point in my whole ministry. It was an introduction to a way of learning-by-doing. This was no easy DIY kit or course pack to take back to the parish. It was an introduction, not to a model to be copied, but to a process in which to be engaged.

Over the following year my own understanding of the process was consolidated through a series of weekend workshops facilitated by the UK New Way of Being Church team at the College of the Ascension, Birmingham. I was very impatient to share my discovery with others so I invited the Marins team (with the goodwill of the Anglican and Roman Catholic bishops) to run a four-day workshop in Plymouth during the summer of 1995, and this was followed by further workshops.

### What are the basic ecclesial communities?

Basic ecclesial communities began in the Roman Catholic Church as a basic way of being church in the social and political context of Latin America. They are not, however, limited to Latin America or to the Catholic Church but exist in many different forms across the world. Here we will confine discussion to Latin America.

**Basic:** A BEC is basic in that it is the smallest unit of being church, existing at the grassroots level of the ordinary people, who are usually the poorest and most marginalised. A BEC contains all the essential elements of being church. The parish is geographically subdivided into a number of BECs, so that a parish becomes a 'community of smaller communities'. The BEC is the point at which the Church as salt, leaven and light engages in the life of the local community.

**Ecclesial:** A BEC is ecclesial in that it embodies the essential elements that make it truly a local expression of the Church. It is an autonomous cell of the Church, yet it is interdependent with the other BECs that make up the parish. It is linked with the diocese and the universal Church through its ordained ministers. In this structure the members participate together in the various ministries that enable the BEC to function. Unlike a traditional group, there is no one leader upon whom everyone else depends. A ministry of coordination is undertaken on behalf of the group by its members in turn. The coordinator is not a leader but someone who links together the various ministries within the BEC.

The parish priest coordinates the mission of the Church at the parish level. He is a visible sign of the unity of the Church at the grassroots level and is the link with the bishop and the wider Church.

**Community:** The BEC is a community of people whose lives are bound up with one another in practical love and service. Each community has the minimum of structure and coordination required to enable the community to function. All the community members are encouraged to participate and they have a strong sense of mutual responsibility.

### Two fundamental characteristics of the BECs

1. *Church as community*: A BEC is made up of a 'human-sized' local community of people who know and support one another. They meet as a small church community, in a home, a local hall or hut, maybe weekly or perhaps fortnightly. They come together with other BECs from time to time for parish events such as a Eucharist (weekly, monthly, depend-

ing upon the availability of the parish priest). They work together on common projects to improve the quality of life for the whole community and to challenge injustice and oppression. Their practice of theology begins with the reality of life as it is experienced. Biblical, prayerful reflection with a view to action is fundamental to their common life as church.

I have met with many BECs in different parts of Brazil, Bolivia, Chile and Argentina and am always struck by the quality of their community life and their generous hospitality. I feel privileged to have experienced something of the ethos of the early Church. Despite the fact that they are among the poorest people in Latin America, these people have a joy and spontaneous generosity that puts us to shame. They certainly know how to celebrate. Fiestas (celebrations) and meals together play an important part in sustaining their common life. One of the words one hears again and again is *esperanza* – hope!

In Latin America 'being church' means above all belonging to a community. In Britain to 'go to church' means to be associated with a particular building. Perhaps the most striking difference between these church communities and our own in Britain is the link between their faith and life. Life is not compartmentalised into sacred and secular. Consequently, political, social, economic and religious issues are all part of the BEC agenda.

There is a robust realism about the worship that I experienced in Latin America. It was certainly not a case of 'Marxism to music'. The hymns and prayers are Christ-centred, Bible-related, and rooted in the reality of everyday experience. In Britain, church groups so often fail to make that connection, and tend to be introspective and escapist. Even if they are outward looking it is usually in terms of evangelism and 'bringing people in' rather than the wider agenda of mission and the reign of God.

2. *Church with the agenda of mission* The fundamental orientation of the BECs is mission. They exist to be agents of change towards the reign of

God. Consequently, every aspect of life is involved – spiritual, social, political, economic, cultural.

The primary concern of Jesus in the Synoptic Gospels is the reign of God. The manifesto he announced in the synagogue in Nazareth (Luke 4:18ff) proclaims good news for the poor and liberation for the oppressed. It is a highly political agenda, and seems to encompass what Jesus meant by the reign of God.

In his three-year public ministry Jesus put this gospel into practice. He spent much of his time with those on the margins of society. He embodied good news to such people. He brought them new life and hope for this life as well as for eternity. At the end of his ministry Jesus passed on his mission to the embryo Church, which became a privileged instrument (but not the only instrument) of the reign of God. It is by its very nature the 'Jesus project' for the world. Fundamental to the very existence of the Church is an orientation to mission.

### Learning from the BECs, and their relevance to Britain

I am often told that because our culture is so very different from that of Latin America their model can have little relevance to us. Of course, we cannot simply transplant the model, and whatever we do here must be appropriate to our culture and context, all applied theology has to be contextual, but there are a number of characteristics that are fundamental to the very nature and mission of the Church and that apply in any context. It is these that are of particular relevance to us. I have to say that in my experience the similarities far outweigh the differences.

I always have a sense of the continuity between the ethos of the early Church and the BECs and this has encouraged me to explore the possibilities for a more authentic and communitarian model of church committed to mission here in England. The BECs have had nearly four decades of practical experience in Latin America. They have shown us that an alternative model for the church is possible.

### Beginning the process in an Anglican parish

Early in the autumn of 1995, following the Manns summer workshops, we started a weekly evening course on a *New Way of Being Church* in which about twenty-five members of St Barnabas were able to take part. The course finished at the end of November, and we decided as a church to take the process forward.

From the start of 1996, the parish was divided into three or four geographical mission areas and in each of these a neighbourhood group was made up of church members and anyone else who lived in the area. The primary purpose of each group was to develop as the basic local unit of the church orientated to mission and the reign of God (that is, with the same purpose as the BECs). Participation in a group by those who lived in other mission areas of the parish was discouraged, though there had to be some flexibility in this.

### Orientation to mission

We now had a practical structure for mission and pastoral care that covered the whole parish and gave a far greater chance of knowing each local neighbourhood and the people who lived there. Indeed, the first stage of mission is to develop an awareness of the neighbourhood, the people and the situations (that is, stage one of the pastoral cycle – see).

> When the members of each BEC met together, they would share stories of the people and situations they had encountered since they had last met together. They would then engage in prayerful reflection on what had happened, using the Bible in order to try to discover 'the word of God for now' and to decide upon any action to be taken (that is,.stages two and three – reflect and act).

> The actions might be very simple – a visit to a bereaved person, attending a community meeting – but I think this is what Jesus meant when he spoke about being salt, light and leaven in the world. It is mission at the simplest level and is a way of mobilising the Church at the grassroots.

> I used to think of mission primarily in terms of personal evangelism. But the mission of Jesus and the Church is much wider than this. And if it

is, then the transformation of all aspects of the world towards the reign of God has to be our concern. For many of us this has meant a radical re-focusing away from the Church and the Church's agenda, to the world and a reign-of-God agenda.

## A different way of using the Bible

The Bible occupies an important place in the life of the BECs, but it is used in a different way, a way that is not intended as an alternative but as an addition to traditional Bible study. In this new way, instead of being the object of study in order to gain knowledge at an individual level, it becomes the subject through which the group discerns God's word for now, with a view to action. Various methods of prayerful reflection have been found useful as tools to enable this to happen. When the neighbourhood groups use the Bible in this new reflective way, they are not dependent upon leaders and teachers.

### How do neighbourhood groups work?

Perhaps the most difficult and necessary change is a change of mind-set from thinking about going to church to being the church. Many parishes have house groups meeting for Bible study, prayer and fellowship. Each group usually has a leader appointed and approved by the vicar. Fellowship, prayer and faith are deepened and mutual support in good times and bad is a real benefit for those who take part. In neighbourhood groups, while recognising that all of these benefits are valuable, the fundamental purpose for which the groups have been set up needs to be grasped by those who participate.

## Ministries within the group

The first and most obvious difference is the way in which a group operates. Different ministries or tasks need to be undertaken to enable it to function smoothly. The following ministries were usually to be found in our groups. The list is neither exhaustive nor prescriptive. We needed to be disciplined in our approach to the working of the groups without being too rigid and without seeing this New Way as a method rather than the development of a fundamentally different process. We can also be so informal that we fail to make the best use of the time we have together as a group.

*Coordination* Ideally the task is shared by a number of coordinators who take it in turns to be responsible to the group for linking together the various elements that make up the time available for the meeting. Our experience has shown that if there is only one coordinator, a group all too easily reverts to the old style of the leader-dependency model.

*Hospitality* Informality and welcome into someone's home play a significant part in the development of their ethos.

*Fiesta/Celebration* The Latin American temperament is much more exuberant than our own, and the ability to have fun, with food, music and dancing, is a marked characteristic of their life together.

*Memory* Each time the group meets someone records a 'memory' of the evening. This consists of one member's perspective on what happened and what actions were decided when the group last met. The next time the group meets the 'memory' is read out. This brings those who were absent up to date and serves as a valuable incentive for the group to carry out the actions decided upon last time and to evaluate those actions that have been taken.

*News* Items of local national and international news from radio, press and television are discussed. This may provide the starting point for biblical reflection.

*Prayer/worship* The BECs and neighbourhood groups are not only groups for social action, but when they meet as church, they are aware of the reality of God and the presence of the Holy Spirit. Thus the spiritual perspective is central to the very existence of the group as it seeks to discern the word of God and to understand what he is saying 'now' to the situations and people that are brought to the attention of the group.

*Time-keeping* The group needs to decide how it is to apportion the time available for memory, reflection, prayer news, etc.

### What about leadership of the parish?

As a vicar I had to learn to work in a new way and to provide a different style of leadership. I began to see my role not so much as leader, but as animator and facilitator of the people. There has sometimes been a conflict between this new role and the strictly legal requirements of the work of a vicar. For several years I did not chair a parochial church council meeting, though I was often present. The result was a growing confidence on the part of the PCCs and a real acceptance of responsibility for the church's life and mission.

If there is to be genuine change, one cannot devolve responsibility and later take it back when difficulties arise. There is a risk and that choice has to be made by the vicar. A vicar may be fortunate, as I was, in having a bishop who trusts him in what he is doing. It is usually easier to ask forgiveness afterwards rather than permission before!

### REFLECT

Looking back on the experience, I would highlight the following:

- This *New Way of Being Church* is not a matter of restructuring the church, though restructuring is inevitably involved. On a superficial level, it may seem to be a question of reorganising the local church into small groups. Certainly the size of a group or community affects the ability of those present to participate, but this is not the essence of the enterprise. It is about a different mind-set for clergy and people in Britain. It involves a way of thinking about *being* church rather than *going* to church. It means leaving behind the deeply ingrained stereotypes of the past.

- For me, *New Way* is energised by a conviction about the rightness of the approach of Liberation Theology and a new understanding of what is meant by the gospel, the reign of God and good news for today, entailing a recognition that the Church's mission is entrusted to the whole people of God, especially those at the grassroots of society. It has a very high theology of the Church as a privileged (but not the only) instrument of the reign of God in the world.

- Since 1996 there has been a natural and almost imperceptible re-direction of our focus towards the local community. Much of the care and involvement with neighbours takes place on an individual spontaneous basis and by its nature cannot be quantified or monitored. But what is different now is a conscious re-focusing outwards to the local community

We have recognised that groups and activities originally set up by the parish no longer have as their ulterior motive 'getting bottoms on pews', but exist because it is kingdom business for us to share with others. Space does not permit to tell the story of growing involvement in the local community but it has meant that as church and non-church people are constantly rubbing shoulders, friendships and relationships are made on a far wider basis than ever before. The Church is taken seriously as non-church people see us taking the community seriously. In fact the 'us and them' boundary has largely disappeared.

- The different way of using the Bible, with reflection on life's reality, is at the very heart of a New Way and perhaps for others this may be the best starting point of a process of re-learning and engaging in mission.
- I have learnt the hard way that to communicate this vision to a parish is not easy. There can be a huge gap between what is said or printed and what people see, hear and understand. There is a fine line between animating people with a vision and imposing new ways upon a resentful church. The people have to own the process. I was perhaps too anxious to restructure the parish into neighbourhood groups before the reflective way of using the Bible (see – reflect – act) had been really established.

## ACT

I long to see the development of a *New Way of Being Church* in England but it will not be achieved by prescribing a programme. Rather, I have tried to encourage a change of mind-set, and to introduce a process and some basic tools for getting from where we are now to where we would like to be.

The *first step* is to recognise that change is urgently needed, and to have a vision for the church of the future.

The *second step* is a recognition that there is no short cut, that there is no programme to follow. Nor must anyone think that this change can be achieved in one great leap forward. Bishop Peter Price's advice is to ask the simple question, 'What is the next achievable step that I can take?'

There is a UK based team which has been helping the development of *A New Way of Being Church* in Britain. We are always willing to advise anyone on ways of initiating the processes described here.[1]

**Notes**

[1] The address is: *A New Way of Being Church*, Wells, Somerset, BA5 2PD, tel. 01749 683143

# 8. Some implications of the Sant'Egidio movement

## TOM GILLUM

What long term responsibilities are we personally willing to take on towards becoming community as well as church?

How do we contribute to a fruitful relationship between the established parish system and the emerging hunger for alternative forms of church life?

*Tom Gillum trained as a solicitor and practised in the field of family law for seven years before ordination in the Church of England. He served his curacy at Holy Trinity, Brompton, and is now Vicar of St Stephen's Church, Westbourne Park, London.*

*He is an enthusiast for the Sant'Egidio movement in Rome and explains here how the Church of England might learn from its experience.*

'Claudio, please help me by explaining what is Sant'Egidio's model?' We were enjoying our second, if not third, cappuccino of the morning, albeit in an hitherto untried café in the Piazza Sant'Egidio in Trastevere. The area has been associated with the Jewish population of Rome and until relatively recently had become run down. Now it is a bustle of life with the narrow streets coming down from the Tiber filled with shoppers, restaurant-goers, tourists and the bustle of city life. Claudio Betti, one of the leaders of the Sant'Edigio community, had been very generous in giving Joanna and me a great deal of his time over the long weekend we had been in Rome. His name had come through a diplomat who, whilst in Rome, had become a friend and supporter of the community.

Plans made in advance with Claudio had all been very relaxed. 'Come and find me at the office on Saturday afternoon – anyone can tell you where I will be.'

When I had asked Claudio if he could let me have something in writing about the community, he had only briefly paused before telling me, 'We put very little into writing.'

Meeting up with Claudio had proved even easier than he had said. We walked through the outer doors of 3a Piazza Sant'Egidio and the gently smiling man behind the switchboard was identified as none other than Claudio. 'Let's go and have a coffee!' He started chatting us through the story of the community.

1968 had been a year of unrest, not least amongst a group of Roman students, including Claudio. Mainly from well-to-do backgrounds, they had become aware of their own ignorance of the large numbers of very poor people (gypsies, migrants from the south of Italy) living on the perimeter of their city, seemingly forgotten by this world. They also saw a wide gap between the Jesus of the Gospels, living close to the poor, and the Jesus worshipped in their historic churches.

So began a 'movement', a community bonded together by a common vision and by a commitment to live and work with the poor, in the name of Jesus. (The 'poor' are probably best defined as those left or allowed to remain on the margins of life.) From these small beginnings, the community grew and now exists not just in Italy (although the largest grouping by far is in Rome), but prospers throughout the world, in Latin and African countries and also in Northern Europe and the USA. It is predominantly a movement among lay people and the number in the community who are priests is minimal.

In our weekend visit to Rome, Joanna and I were to witness some of the lasting effects of 1968, shaped by the distinctive hand of Jesus Christ.

'We do not have a model. We are an experience.' As Claudio spoke to us, it became clear that the heart of Sant'Egidio is friendship. 'The poor are our friends – we spend time together and develop friendship.'

I liked the sound of this – it took us away from unhelpful and patronising approaches to 'the poor'. On our first evening Claudio had taken us to meet a youth group, just round the corner from their restaurant for the poor. We could see there was a strong bond of friendship between him and the leader. We saw the same friendship at the restaurant (a pleasant café where large numbers are served a meal each evening). It was all very relaxed, and people clearly came first.

It would, I felt, be wrong simply to explain the priority given to friendship and, indeed, the ease of friendship in terms of 'the Latin temperament'. I could not help being challenged to face the possibility that my question about Sant'Egidio's 'models' may have revealed an tendency in me to (unwittingly) exaggerate organisation and administration at the expense of basic human relationships. (Sant'Egidio do have an administrative base, but no one is paid to work there.) Even more importantly, without this emphasis on friendship, it may well be that neither a true understanding nor an experience of God's friendship can be appreciated and enjoyed.

The Church of Santa Maria in Trastevere is one of the (many) jewels of Rome. It dominates the piazza adjacent to Sant'Egidio. The facade was beautifully lit when we approached the church at 8.30 on Saturday evening and as we joined the flow of others coming for the community's night prayer we found ourselves with a sense of anticipation.

This church was the original venue for the worship that lies at the heart of the community's common life. Their overriding emphasis is on the transforming power of the gospel of Jesus Christ. Within the context of human frailty and apparent insignificance, there is high confidence that the grace of God works in and through ordinary people.

Today, in over twenty places in Rome, members of the community join together to place themselves under the gospel and to bring their prayers to the throne of grace. They have developed their own liturgy in which the psalm of the day and other parts of the service are sung. Emphasis is placed on biblical exposition of the gospel.

As we entered the church on that Saturday evening, we were greeted by the gentle sound of a small singing group. Claudio sat next to us and in a hoarse whisper translated the talk for us. (There is also a translating facility through the more efficient if less personal medium of headsets.) Towards the end of the service there was extempore prayer.

It was a captivating experience to join in the worship in that place where spirituality and social action meet. The service is open to anyone and many people in Rome who do not belong to the community attend the worship. The emphasis, however, is very much on those who are making friendships with the poor and placing themselves under the gospel regularly, if not daily.

'Which football team do you support?' The eleven-year-old boy looked back at me as if doubting whether we came from the same planet. It was now Monday afternoon and we were in the basement of a nursery school in the suburbs of Rome. The experience of the early (or perhaps not so early) rush hour traffic had been memorable as Luca, a member of the community, drove us to the after-school club (*scuola populare*) we were to visit. About a dozen children had gathered to do their homework, to reflect on the place of the death penalty in today's world and to continue friendship with the three community members who commit themselves to the scuola for three hours each weekday evening.

We learnt that the home circumstances of these children were difficult and all were deprived to a greater or lesser extent. At home, the children received little or no affirmation and there was a singular lack of basic relational opportunity. We heard of a gradual flowering and emergence from their shells as the children made friends and grew in confidence. Opportunities had been opened for them to express themselves and hitherto undetected talents had been revealed. The effects had not been limited to the children; real changes had also been brought to parents and grandparents. The transforming power of the gospel was there before us – made possible by friendship.

The commitment of the adult helpers was remarkable. Work patterns in Rome are different from those in London. The working day starts earlier and, for some, ends soon after lunch. Part-time work is more frequent than in

London. To give three hours a day (with travel on top of that) to service a *scuola populare* was a powerful statement of what it meant to be disciples of Jesus Christ. I could not think of many in London who are doing this without any financial remuneration.

When we left the after-school club, one of the helpers went off in a different direction to join in one of the services with a predominance of younger people (under thirty years old) but the other two made the journey back to Trastevere for night prayer. There we again received strength for the work to which we were called as we listened to the gospel and its application to our lives and as we joined with the church in prayer. This is the time when the weary and heavy-laden are able to cast the burden of the work on to the One who gives rest and whose yoke is light.

## REFLECTION[1]

The Sant'Egidio community challenges our own ecclesiology and understanding of the gospel. As I reflect on all I have learned, it seems to me that the theology is far more radical than may at first sight be apparent. Some points stand out.

### Mission
Mission fuelled by the love of God is at the forefront of the work. The gospel must be lived out in everyday life; compassion must move through into action.

### The poor
It is the poor who draw us close to the heart of God, and it is by befriending and serving the poor that we can become givers and receivers of the gospel. Each member is expected to get involved with something, even if only once a month, perhaps serving in the soup kitchen, cleaning toilets or sorting out clothes. Anyone joining the community is drawn in to working with the poor as quickly as is possible, and is thus taken right into the heart of Sant'Edidio (but individual initiative to start a new project is only encouraged when a person has been involved in the community for some time).

### The gospel

Actions born of hearts touched by God's love for the poor speak of the truths of the gospel. These gospel truths – the grace and love of God, transformation and hope – are most likely to be articulated in the exposition at night prayer and in discussion at a fellowship meeting. There are also 'schools of the gospel', designed for people who are far from the gospel, where the word of God is listened to.

### Friendship

Friendship – when people are readily accepted for who they are – is taken seriously and is the guarantee that fellowship remains at the centre of the Community's life. But friendship is not an end in itself – it needs to move on to true fellowship. Good intentions held by like-minded people cannot of themselves bring about this true fellowship. Mutual engagement with the poor (and in the reflective process arising from this) is the avenue by which a friendship moves on to the next phase. St Paul understood this. The fellowship is 'in Christ', in the work of the gospel, and so demands a shared participation in the life of Christ.

### Community

Sant'Egidio makes an important contribution to the Church's understanding of what may be meant today by the word 'community' in the cities of the Western world. Rather than trying to live together under one roof ('We found living together very difficult!' conceded Claudio), community is seen as a network of relationships centred on discipleship. This recognises the restrictions of housing in many of our cities as well as the various contexts (work, social life, family) which many today have to try to hold together. The Sant'Egidio approach offers flexibility while maintaining a focus on the purpose of community: a living out of the gospel.

### Organisation

There is a non-authoritarian atmosphere. Meetings are run by coordinators and not leaders and there is no rigid, set agenda.

### Worship

Numbers in themselves do not prove anything, but the many who attend night prayer are a powerful testimony to the fact that a daily coming together before God is deeply embedded in the life of Sant'Egidio. In addition, every Saturday, there is celebration of the Eucharist. The Community's worship is its own, expressed in distinctive ways, but it draws heavily upon the Church's experience of prayer down the years. In the path they tread, the community recognises that they are and must remain linked to the whole, but are at the same time a prophetic voice just inside it.

## DISCIPLESHIP

The Sant'Egidio community offers the Church a way of discipleship that synthesises worship, fellowship and mission. It may be helpful to reflect on the structures that the community would see itself as providing and those that would be provided by the wider Church. At the risk of being simplistic, the following analysis of discipleship in a modern urban setting is offered.

### Church

Healthy discipleship needs opportunities for worship that take people beyond the boundaries of familiarity and comfort. Simply to meet always with a group who worship in the 'right' or the 'best' way is likely ultimately to lead to idolatry. Diversity is part of the reality of the Church and therefore to join in with the worship of the Church (most probably involving some sort of compromise) connects us to the Church as it is, and thereby to ourselves as we are and to God as he is. Gathering on a Sunday with a grouping who, either because of geographical proximity, relational links, or for a host of other reasons, happen to be present, is something many are likely to kick against, but such worship is a vital part of a bigger picture and states to the world at large the priority of God in our world. Within the context of the Church of England, the parish church is ideally suited to fulfil this role.

### Community

The second grouping that every disciple needs is a community. This is a grouping that is capable of nurturing people in their discipleship. It must be small enough to be cohesive and to provide relational support. It could be an extended biological family, a home group (not necessarily restricted to any one local church), or a group based around the workplace or an area of practical involvement. In Rome, a Sant'Egidio fellowship group might be such a community. Words such as healing, hospitality, trust, openness and love are likely to be central. Everyone should know that they belong to a community – and should not aim to belong to more than one.

### Network

The Sant'Egidio community challenges us to place mission at the forefront of discipleship. Neither the parish church nor a community (as defined above) may offer the best structure for mission, though some may. The parish priest, however, has all too often to focus on pastoral work and in few local churches are there sufficient numbers of people with enough motivation to sustain social projects. The emphasis of a community is most naturally the nurture of an individual's own growth. Though it should be expected that a degree of natural missionary activity should flow from healthy nurture, in practice, the structure through which mission is most easily able to happen is a 'network' based on friendship and common interests.

### The locus for discipleship.

The community also challenges us to question the place of the parish church as the only locus for discipleship. Within the Church of England, this is a central issue. It is easy to assume that a local church is, and should be, providing the necessary structures and opportunity for discipleship. The parish has long been seen as the primary context in which discipleship of Jesus is expected to be worked out. In practice, however, the extent to which many believers actually engage in worship, fellowship and mission often depends on an active parish church, usually an active vicar. The shortcomings of this preconception are all too apparent.

In the experience of the Sant'Egidio community, the small group is the primary and crucial unit. This may well be a radical concept for the Church of England. Here is a structure that is not within the organisational chart of the denomination. Where, then, does authority lie? Many parish priests may find it difficult to work alongside a structure that is neither under their control nor directly answerable to the bishop.

The Sant'Egidio community sees friendship as the key, a friendship expressed as company and support for those in the often complex life of parishes today. Members of the community are complementary to the parishes where priests are often overburdened (not least by administration). They describe themselves as a 'house close by', to help the parishes and certainly not an institution to rival them. The friendship is seen first as a friendship of prayer, then one within the 'schools of the gospel', and, of course, also of service of the poor.

### The Church in Britain

Church life in this country already has (in addition to the parish) a range of support structures, be they long-established organisations (like the Bible Society,) para-church bodies or diocesan organisations. Some operate within an individual parish, some within a cluster of commitments, or an ecumenical fraternal. What, therefore, is another such organisation likely to offer other than further confusing the picture, if not leading to even deeper fragmentation?

In my view, the Sant'Egidio community undoubtedly offers much to the Church. Its theological emphases are simple, memorable and are capable of opening up a fullness of the gospel. It has a coherent theology in which worship, mission and fellowship are inter-bound. In particular, it walks in an ancient gospel tradition that puts compassionate mission back into the heart of the life of the Church and does it in a way that makes it a mission in which everyone can (and must) participate.

Much of this could happen (and, of course, in places it is happening) in many of our churches, not least in the Church of England. Sant'Egidio challenges us to reflect more deeply, not least on the relationship between community and parish.

'Sant'Egidio does not have a model; we are an experience.' That statement reveals the community's greatest strength and takes us to the heart of what it offers the rest of the Church. Any organisation that wishes to reproduce itself risks that either clones will emerge, which ultimately lack the creativity and vitality that gave birth to their parents, or worse, that ossification will set in. Where once there was real life, instead only memory is perpetuated.

It was in this spirit that Sant'Egidio was born. In this same spirit a Church such as ours should respond to the challenge before us.

---

**Notes**

[1]  Andreas Riccardi, the founder of the Sant'Egidio community, has allowed a series of his interviews with J. D. Durand and R. Ladous to be published (*Sant'Egidio, Rome and the World*, St Paul's Press, 1996) This sets out his perception of the Community and his own priorities and burdens. Anyone interested to find out more may be sent a copy, but those who ask for copies will first be urged to come to Rome, where they will see for themselves, as they meet warm hospitality, plenty of laughter and responses to their questions.

# 9. The story (so far) of DNA Networks

## JANIE AND DAVID BEALES

When we encounter a successful new model for how things can be done, the temptation is to import it in its entirety into our local situation: how do we discern what is relevant?

Can we see in our own church history those building blocks that are worth holding on to as we seek to embrace change?

*David Beales had been a diocesan evangelist in Melbourne (Australia) before he and his wife, Janie, returned to England in 2000. What they are now doing in and around Colchester, Essex, makes for exciting reading. Here they tell the story.*

### BACKGROUND

Together we lead DNA Networks, which is a church-planting movement. We seek to work within the historic denominations and value cooperative unity among the churches.

In the year 2000 we returned from Melbourne to Colchester, Essex. David's mother had recently been widowed and we felt a happy responsibility to live nearby. Indeed, through late 1998 and 1999 our spirits had been stirred to live and work in Colchester. We believed that it was time to integrate our spiritual gifts and concluded that a church-planting ministry was the most appropriate way of expressing the mix of our talents and spirituality. Further, we believed that we were to be catalysts to the planting of a network of worshipping communities in Colchester, East Anglia, Australia and other nations.

## PARADIGM SHIFTS

We had spoken frequently of the shifting mission paradigms facing the followers of Jesus. It was time to stop talking about it; we felt the imperative to shift a paradigm! We set up a partnership bank account called 'Paradigm Shifters' and bought a house a few stone throws away from the mother of the Constantine paradigm shift! I'm talking of St Helena, the mother of the Emperor Constantine, who is reputed to have been born in Colchester. Helena stands on top of the town hall as the town's patron saint, holding high the 'true cross' which she claimed to have found in Jerusalem.

The Emperor Constantine Christianised the Roman Empire and thereby ended the apostolic mission paradigm of the first three centuries. While we can mutter about the problems of Church-State links, mergers of military and mission interests and Christendom's subsequent abuses of power, the edict of Constantine was great news for the followers of Jesus who lived in Colchester. Within a few years of that edict, after centuries of persecution, they had built a place for worship in Colchester. The remnants of this worship centre's ancient walls, discovered in the 1980s, can still be seen beside the new police station. Indeed, these fourth- century remains represent the earliest surviving evidence of a place of Christian worship in these islands. Where better to shift a paradigm than the place that spawned an earlier paradigm shift?

## DNA NETWORKS

So we created a charitable trust named Dynamic New Anglian Networks. Why this name?

- We wanted to be flexible enough to interact with our culture – hence dynamic; we also wanted to be powered by the dynamic of the Spirit.
- We realised that we had to create something new; Jesus spoke of new wineskins, but he also spoke of the householder taking out treasures both old and new. In creating something that did not formerly exist, we sought also to draw on the wells of two millennia of living stories and spirituality.
- We were called to East Anglia.

- We recognised that most people seek their identities in networks of relationships (work, leisure, family, friends) prior to any acknowledgement of those geographical localities we refer to as parish boundaries.

DNA contains the genetic fingerprints of life. DNA Networks seeks to embody and multiply the fingerprints of Jesus. Together with the dynamic of the Spirit, incarnation and multiplication are key theological paradigms for us. Acts 1:8 fired our imagination and faith: 'You will receive power when the Holy Spirit comes on you; and you will be my witnesses in Jerusalem, and in all Judea and Samaria, and to the ends of the earth' (NIV) .

We heard this text ask us a question so we entered into a dialogue:

'Do you believe what Jesus said to his apostles?'

'Yes!'

'Is there any reason why the same promise does not apply to you?'

'No!'

'Go on then!'

'But this might not be in the denomination's five-year-plan... we haven't got all the money in place... what will other churches think?'

I imagined myself making all these excuses at the throne on the Last Day. A gentle voice would reply, 'Which part of the word "Go" did you not understand?'

### Walls, wells and waiting

It takes thirty minutes to complete a brisk walk around the ancient Roman wall of Colchester. During 2000, we prayer-walked the walls virtually every weekday. Gradually, we came to appreciate the spiritual wells that had been dug by our ancestors. The ancient Roman church beside the police station; the ruins of St Botolph's Priory, the first Augustinian Priory in Britain; the martyrs killed in the 1550s during the paradigm shift known as the Reformation; and up the road across the river from Mersea Island, the chapel of St Peter, built as a missionary base by St Cedd in the seventh century. These ancient remains, memories and monuments all told stories of faith and witness in earlier days. The prayers of the saints seemed still to be currents of hope reverberating in the air and touching us with encouragement.

> As we walked the walls and read the history, we were changed. We came to love the land and to feel a deep sense of provocation in our spirits. Paul was provoked by the idols in Athens. We were provoked by the message sent by the redundant church buildings of Colchester. Instead of the living fulfilment of Acts 1:8, the witness of the town centre is that the Church is now redundant, a heritage issue, and its God has taken early retirement! Museums, an arts centre, a masonic centre, empty shells; the spiritual heritage of two millennia seemed to be like blocked wells.
>
> While we walked walls and noticed wells, we waited. This was difficult for an activist – until we stumbled on Scripture: 'Since ancient times no-one has heard, no ear has perceived, no eye has seen any God besides you, who acts on behalf of those who wait for him' (Isaiah 64:4 NIV).

We noticed that Isaiah's prophecies of return from exile were full of God making things 'spring up'. We waited and remained on the lookout to see what God would cause to spring up in Colchester.

**Spring-up**

While we longed for the DNA of Jesus to grow into a body, we didn't design the shape of the body. We believe in church planting not cloning. We found that, first, people with passions sprang up, then finances, then mission.

> We met Manik Corea, who arrived in Colchester from Singapore via America. A Singaporean, Manik had been an international student in London in the 1990s. He spoke of his concern for international students in England. Then we discovered that Essex University, just outside Colchester, had the highest concentration of internationals in the country. During the summer of 2000, I introduced Manik to Enoch

Kunarajah, whom I had met at Colchester Cricket Club. Enoch is a Sri Lankan Christian studying for a Ph D at Essex. Manik and Enoch began to pray together.

Our son Shane had gone to Colchester Sixth Form College. Within a few weeks of moving into our house in Colchester, Shane and three friends had brought fifteen people home for an Alpha Course. We worked with the students to prepare the talks and facilitate the small groups – and we provided a kitchen for making pizzas. At the end, we booked the Colchester Arts Centre for a celebration concert at which Alpha participants were interviewed about their experiences of the course. On the night, 184 people showed up, largely because several members of a popular local band were on the Alpha Course and played at the event.

We met Baptist minister Terry Tennens. Terry was at that time working in business and had developed a concern for mission and ministry at the workplace. His passion was to practise a biblical approach to being a Christian at work. We invited Terry to come and pray with us and mingle with us. As he did, he developed a vision for a new workplace ministry in Colchester.

At the same time, we knew a family who had moved to the area from London. We visited them and prayed with them a few times, sharing a vision for planting in 2001. When the time came, they joined us.

**Mission units**
Each of these 'spring-ups' became the origin of a mission unit. A mission unit is not a church or a congregation. It is an intention to do mission among a particular group of people. The goal of the mission units is to create a community of faith in Jesus.

The paradigm shift is simple. Whereas in the church paradigm, church gives shape to mission, in the mission paradigm, mission gives shape to church. Much church planting is church cloning[1], springing out of the church paradigm. Take between twenty and seventy people out of an existing church and they'll usually plant a church that looks like the one from which they came.

Missionary church planting is like giving birth. An expectant couple will not know what the new person will look like, but they know something of the DNA that has created the new person. They know what they and their parents and grandparents look like. Nor will they know the precise circumstances in which they will parent their child. They'll do the best they can with the resources they have of love and care and wisdom and material goods.

### A worship community
By mid-2001, four mission units were functioning:
- internationals
- young adults
- workers
- families with pre-schoolers.

On Trinity Sunday, 10 June 2001, we gathered twenty-one people together to worship God. We met in a leisure centre at 5 p.m. and called the event Live at Five.

During June 2002, we celebrated the first birthday of Live at Five with a week of activities. We remembered what had happened over the twelve months and set our faces to continue in mission into the future. During the week, thirty-five people came on Wednesday to the prayer dedication of the office and meeting room we had recently rented; sixty came on Thursday to a retreat day in the country; forty-five came on Saturday to the young adults Identity event; a total of sixty came to the two Sunday services of worship at the Arena Leisure Centre. Live at Five currently attracts sixty regular participants; twice as many take part in ongoing groups and events run by the mission units. Probably 75 per cent of these were not involved in any local church before they participated with us. Many are on their way towards becoming followers of

Jesus. Others have chosen to follow Jesus during the year.

We prefer that people don't 'transfer' from their church to us. Those from other churches who are called to serve in mission with us can be either seconded or sent, as are overseas missionaries.

**What do we value?**
DNA is so complex and intricate that if a person's DNA were stretched out entirely it would reach from the earth to the moon. Unravelling our spiritual DNA also generates a lengthy list of values. We have sought to give expression to these values. I hope that our behaviour and communal life gives them away.

Since we aim to embody and multiply the fingerprints of Jesus, we take Jesus' own manifesto (Luke 4:19) as the basis of our mission. Our mission goals are:

- to communicate good news to the poor, glimpses of God, the favour of God;
- to heal the broken-hearted;
- to set people free to pursue their godly dreams.

*We believe in God's mission in the world*: therefore we value the whole community in which we are placed. Believing that we are called to operate the 'Heineken Principle' ('to reach the parts that other beers cannot reach'), we seek to serve people around us from many nations (including students, immigrants and refugees) and those who have no commitments to a local church.

*We believe in evangelising community*: therefore we value worship evangelism[2]. We communicate the message of the gospel; we invite people into community life; we share our communion with God.

'Communicate', 'community', 'communion' – three 'com' words. 'Com' means 'with', so we conclude that evangelism is a 'with' word more than a 'to' word. While we seek to equip individuals to speak about their reasons for faith and their story of faith, we recognise the dynamic of the Spirit present in the community of disciples. We seek to make our worship accessible and excellent, yet we have faith that God touches people in preaching, reading Scripture, testimony, prayers, prophetic revelation, worship arts, silence and sacrament.

*We believe in ministry teams*: therefore we value the inclusion of new (and older) followers of Jesus, as well as and those on their way towards Christ, in teams for service where they work according to their giftedness. For example, four gap-year students, two of whom had become Christians in the previous year, have resourced the leadership of our young adults work. Our young adult volunteers have included quite a few who do not own Christian faith yet desire to serve the community.

*We believe in one-to-one mentoring*, particularly for seekers and new followers of Jesus, therefore we value training for disciplers. A common mentoring pattern is to meet for one hour and to spend twenty minutes catch-up and storytelling; twenty minutes of reading the Bible in response to issues and stories raised; twenty minutes in prayer (including silent prayer) springing out of the issues and the Bible passage.

*We believe in small groups*: therefore we value some of the cell church principles. We are not a pure cell church: our mission units are sometimes group based and sometimes not. We seek, however, to initiate and mobilise holistic small groups that are relational, biblical, prayerful and open to include and serve outsiders.

*We believe in global multiplication*: therefore we value training for potential church planters. We look out for people who may be called to lead a church planting team in the future and encourage them to observe, participate and learn with us. We value theological training integrated with church planting experience. We are currently sending a potential Chinese church planter for part-time study at London Bible College. We will also deploy him as a staff member on our international team.

*We believe in the sacramental character of marriage*: therefore we value the cooperation and integration of couples in ministry. We do not insist on this, since we recognise the value of single people in ministry and honour the individual whose spouse does not want to be included. However, we take the view that a marriage is like a mini-church, where Christ-centred love, trust, mutual submission and as-long-as-you-shall-live loyalty is a sign of the Kingdom of God[3].

*We believe in indiscriminate grace* or *'the Cornelius household factor'*: therefore we value the healthy spiritual experiences of unchurched people. The Holy Spirit fell spontaneously upon the Gentiles in Cornelius' house (Acts 10). Since Peter and Joel both spoke of the Spirit being poured out 'on all flesh', we anticipate, pray for and expect both dramatic and undramatic manifestations of the Spirit's encounter with people who don't know much about Jesus. Visions of Jesus, dreams, revelation of truth, trembling limbs, beating hearts, 'butterflies' in the stomach, instant deliverance from extreme pain have all happened to people we would define as 'unchurched' or 'seekers' in purposefully non-emotional and unhyped environments. The indiscriminate nature of grace continues to sneak up on us and overturn our sacred cows.

*We believe in mustard-seeds of faith to move mountains of finance*: therefore we value the spiritual gift of financial contribution, mentioned by Paul (Romans 12:8) and by Luke (Luke 8:3). Further, we value the partnership of intercessors who know about issues for prayer, including financial needs. We began the work without stipend or financial assurances. Funds have sprung up from individual donors and grant-making bodies. To be strictly honest, this came as a surprise. I thought I'd probably get a job in the Church of England structure but it didn't work out. (No complaints!) We appear still to be a long way from self-sufficiency as a community of faith. My hunch is that we will be self-sufficient after four to eight years. I base this hunch on research by John Finney[4], who found that the average unchurched British adult takes four years to become committed to serve Christ in the fellowship of a local church. At this point, he or she is unlikely to be positioned financially to contribute a tithe; it may take a further period, up to four years, to come to this level of liberality.

## The current shape of DNA Networks

| | |
|---|---|
| Colchester | four mission units and two worship events |
| Partnerships East Anglia: | Tendring Villages Project led by Simon Coleman |
| Europe: | Donau Gemeinde, Lauingen, Bavaria, led by Michael Mack |
| USA: | King of Kings, Charlotte, North Carolina, led by Jon Shuler. |

## Future plans[5]

- to establish ongoing leadership teams to grow forward each mission unit;
- to create one new mission unit/worship event: Sacred Space;
- to catalyse partnership church plants in Australia;
- to prepare to catalyse new church plants in East Anglia and in Asia.

### Notes

[1] See Stuart Murray, *Church Planting, Laying Foundations*, Paternoster, 1998, for further discussion about the difference between planting and cloning.

[2] See *Worship Evangelism, Inviting Unbelievers into the Presence of God*, Sally Morgenthaler, Zondervan, 1995, for further discussion on the theology and practice of the function of worship in the evangelising community.

[3] We are indebted to the work of Dr Jack Dominian for this view. He had written briefly about this in a chapter on marriage and marital breakdown in Jack Dominian and Hugh Montefiore, *God, Sex and Love*, SCM/Trinity Press International, 1989.

[4] John Finney, *Finding Faith Today*, British and Foreign Bible Society, 1992.

[5] For further up-to-date information about what is happening, visit our website at www.dnanetworks.org

# 10. Fires of Heaven

## HUGH ELLIS

Is it possible that in the parish history books there are clues to how change could be implemented while maintaining continuity?

How do we seek civic involvement in the debate on change – one which with sensitivity and creativity would encourage all sections in the community to take some responsibility for the spiritual health of the area?

*Hugh Ellis trained as an RAF pilot and then flew operationally as a navigator before becoming Rector of Bradfield and Stanford Dingley in Berkshire. He is a diocesan clergy work consultant and a member of the Oxford Diocesan Strategy Group for new church models. Here he shares how and why his and neighbouring parishes might move towards a 'monasterium'[1] model for ministry...*

### A STORY

In 1984, while serving in the Royal Air Force as a navigator on Nimrod Maritime Reconnaissance aircraft, I was involved in the leadership of a group of Christians of different denominations who met together for prayer, worship and fellowship. The group existed as the fruit of a thought I had on my posting to 201 Nimrod Squadron, RAF Kinloss, in the summer of 1981. It was this as I perceived it: God was calling his people who were posted to this Station to meet and worship together as the 'Body of Christ' on the Base. Up until that time, only a (relatively) few Christians had attended the Anglican Base church; most went to the church and denomination of their choice sometimes as far as thirty-five miles away. As a consequence, the 'fire of faith' on the Base did not burn as brightly as it might have done.

My wife Jenny and I invited to supper all the Christians we knew who worked on the Station to discuss the 'thought'. It was well received in principle, but bringing the idea into being proved more difficult than we had anticipated. For a year just six of us met in the Station's Anglican church, and 'all' we did was pray and sing one or two songs.

At the end of the year, we became quite despondent, feeling that the vision was good in principle but unachievable in practice. As a result, we did some research on the spiritual life in the area over the preceding fifty years and discovered that during this period there had been a poor track record of Christian fellowship. Many groups had begun but had not lasted for long. The Hebridian revival of the 1950s had moved through to this area of Scotland but for some reason had not touched the Kinloss vicinity, appearing to have avoided the area by some twenty miles. This seemed strange and we wondered about it.

Christians had recently begun to reflect on the concept of 'healing the land'[2]. It was certainly the case that witchcraft, in its various forms, had been openly practised in the local area, but we were unable to ascertain whether there was a link between the witchcraft and the revival's avoidance of this area. We resolved, however, to commit ourselves to a weekend of prayer for the area. That was in the October and by December another couple had a sense of calling to join us in prayer. They were civilians from about ten miles away who had learned of this small prayer cell through their neighbour, who was one of the Nimrod aircrew.

After Christmas, someone new joined us more or less weekly until there were over forty meeting for prayer, worship and fellowship, some coming in from up to thirty-five miles away. At the time it did not seem an unusual phenomenon, even though speakers (through relational links) asked to visit us from around the country and from as far away as Australia. In short, the cell had become a prayer-centred, mission-focused relational network of people committed to the core purpose of prayer-centred mission.

During this period, we discovered that people were praying for us in America. I did not ever discover how they knew of this prayer cell and only found out about them when a letter came, addressed to the group, saying that in prayer for us they had seen a 'vision' (I cannot remember in what form it was perceived). The vision showed sparks emanating from this area of Scotland to England, and where the sparks landed a small fire was started. Although the fires remained small, their hot embers spread until they met with those of other fires. The result was that the country caught alight and the fire eventually leapt the English Channel.

We did not know what to make of the 'vision' but simply held it in our hearts and continued to pray. After three and a half years we sensed that the work of that cell was complete and that we were being called to focus our efforts within the Base Anglican church. Some members of the group were posted to other RAF stations, and some went to different off-base churches, again up to thirty-five miles away. As far as RAF Kinloss was concerned, a spiritual fire was burning, resulting in a significant interest in Christianity and the development of a lively Anglican congregation, facilitated by some excellent chaplains. Since that time, I have learned that similar visions have been experienced by other groups throughout the country, one of which is recounted by Jean Darnall[3].

### Prayer cells and networks

What has this to do with the Church of England and where it is going? In recent years I have become aware of a growing movement of prayer-focused, mission-oriented networks, many of which appear to have originated in the Church of England, although the networks themselves comprise people of various denominations and church groups. These 'fires' take many forms and cross the age spectrum. What the networks have in common is a rhythm of prayer (for the nation or the locality in which they are set), a mission focus and a deep friendship between those committed to a particular prayer cell or network.

This phenomenon is increasingly being described as 'modern monasticism'. Many participants are committing themselves to a rule of life. An increasing number have become Franciscan tertiaries or Benedictine oblates. A small, local, 'fragile' Benedictine community may well have over 350 oblates.

Let me tell you an aspect of our own story here at Bradfield in Berkshire.

### Prayer for Reading

I think, for me, the story began in February 1997 at a Reading church leaders' day of prayer when I was moved to the core as Christian leaders from various denominations were united in a gracious spirit of prayer for Reading. During this time of prayer I was deeply stirred by the simple thought of the Church of England being called to facilitate Christian unity by initiating opportunities for mission-focused prayer. Somehow unity among the diverse expressions of the faith in our local area would be brought about as we prayed together. Since then church leaders have formed the Reading Christian Network. Once a week they meet to have breakfast, to pray and to work together for mission in the Reading area.

### Bradfield

When I became Rector of Bradfield I heard rumours that in the past the church had been connected in some way with monasticism. I was told that a verger had seen what appeared to be a monk dressed in black walking in the churchyard. The verger had called out, but when he caught up with the figure, it disappeared.

At the beginning of Lent 1998, Bradfield PCC agreed, on the suggestion of one of the parishioners, to open the parish church and keep the heating on to facilitate daily lunchtime prayer until Easter. This experience of daily prayer in the church was sufficiently special to lead us to ask whether the practice should continue.

Whilst on leave immediately after Easter, I awoke one morning at 2 a.m. with a deep conviction that I should start each day in prayer at the parish church. This made a good deal of sense to me since I found praying the office in my study difficult because of the distraction of the pressing work on my desk. During the following week, as I turned on the church lights each morning I found myself smiling and reflected that this experience was, to my surprise, rather delightful. In that beautiful and focused context engagement in deep prayer came more easily than in my office.

Before long, I began to sense a calling to 'come in deeper'. It seemed like an invitation into the unknown. It was as though I was standing by a calm Scottish loch on a hot and still summer's day, desiring to bathe in the cool and refreshing waters, yet holding back because the loch was deep and dark. Although the morning is not my best time of day, and although I was certainly unaware of any particular emotion but simply said the daily office (using Celebrating Common Prayer) and waited in silence, I began to encounter God in a deeper way than I had previously known.

I found that my hands began to shake, but only as I engaged in the office. It took a few months to convince myself that I was not experiencing the first stages of Parkinson's disease or the like, but was, somehow, encountering the deep presence of God. A number of others involved in this ministry of prayer are also experiencing something similar. It is a phenomenon that seems mainly to occur during times of prayer when people are leading worship and praying the office.

In May 1998, the PCC agreed that the church should remain open each day and should be heated continually. Although this costs around an extra £1,000 a year the money is well spent. The church is now always relatively comfortable to sit in for lengthy periods. It has ceased to feel damp and there is a welcoming environment for visitors. Somehow, this daily prayer has also affected the atmosphere of the church; many have commented on the deep sense of peace in the church and have felt constrained to worship.

In January 1999, Bradfield PCC discussed whether God had brought forth the ministry of a 'house of prayer' at St Andrew's, Bradfield, and it was agreed that 9 and 10 February should be spent in prayer, waiting on God for clarification. In the stillness, the attention of a number of people was drawn to the idea of monks and subsequently they asked if there had ever been monks here. I said that there had been rumours but we had no evidence. There was also a deep sense of being drawn towards Celtic Christian community, though at that time we had no idea what that comprised.

In the following week, a member of the church discovered from records in Reading Reference Library that for five years in the seventh century Bradfield Church had been the seat of one of the monasteries out of which Abingdom Abbey had been formed. This link was later confirmed by Abingdon Abbey's own records. We also discovered that Bradfield Church had been consecrated by three Irish missionary bishops.

During the following months a number of other 'mystical' (I think that is the best description) phenomena occurred in this restored 'house of prayer'. My sense is that somehow through the daily prayer, the 'veil' between heaven and earth has become thin.

## 'RE-DIGGING THE ANCIENT WELLS'

During the times of prayer there came a recurring thought that the prayer was a sort of re-digging of an ancient well. It brought thoughts of 'the well of life' or the source of the 'river of life' flowing from the throne of God. It was as though the prayers somehow released the life of God into the unconscious life of the community and brought irrigation to the dry spiritual ground of our local culture. Our midday prayers were focused on healing for the sick and I was reminded that in Ezekiel's and John's vision of the river of life, the 'leaves of the trees were for the healing of the nations' (Ezekiel 47:12; Revelation 22:1-2).

During that period, I discovered that members of some Reading Free Churches and house churches were researching the ancient sites of prayer with a sense that God was calling them to 're-dig Abraham's wells' (Genesis 26:15-19). This surprised me since at the time some of the local house churches seemed to want to have nothing to do with anything traditional. I also found that when given the choice of a place for worship, many local young people had chosen to use modern contemplative forms in ancient buildings. Is this a move of the Spirit, or a cultural effect, or both?

A 'modern monasticism movement'[4] is developing, networking those being called to forms of being church that have a rhythm of prayer and rule of life at its heart. This modern form of monasticism is not cloistered but is more Celtic in style or, perhaps, more like that of St Martin of Tours in the fourth century. This does not seem to be a rural phenomenon only. Its principles are being worked out in large evangelical churches such as St Thomas, Crookes, Sheffield, where a five-fold daily rhythm of prayer has been established.

For us here at Bradfield, the vision has developed towards a mission to the gentle stream of pilgrims who visit the church. A creative arts aspect is developing with stained-glass workshops, and it is hoped that we may be able to develop a small retreat centre to facilitate a ministry of hospitality. The concept has extended to our deanery's pastoral plan in which, in partnership with two neighbouring benefices, we hope to explore a new church model, known locally as the 'hub' model. At the heart of this model is what Ian Bradley calls a 'monasterium'[5]. In this model, all ministry begins and ends with prayer; the ministry team members voluntarily commit themselves to a daily rhythm of prayer and rule of life. They become, therefore, more fully Christian community.

Locally, this model is being developed so that the ministry team comprise local ministers (mostly non stipendiary, ecumenical and lay, diverse in spirituality/gifts) with pastoral and leadership responsibility for one community in the 'hub' area.

## SUMMARY

In this story we have moved along way from the prayer/fellowship group at RAF Kinloss, yet the same principles have been at work throughout – Christians meeting and working together in a prayer-centred, mission-focused, relational way of being church. In these days of rapid sociological change I am convinced that God is bringing forth new ways of being church so that his gospel can most effectively reach the people of today's culture. In a society in which Christian lifestyles have become indistinct from the local culture, I believe that God is calling his people to be in community, bound together by a common rule of life that includes a daily pattern of prayer, a core purpose of mission for the extension of God's kingdom on earth and an authentic lifestyle that embodies the values of Christ's teaching.

Throughout history, whenever the Church has become slack in its distinctiveness, monastic communities have arisen. This pattern appears to be returning in our day under the prompting of the Holy Spirit. Whether in the form of cell group or monastic community, the fires of heaven are burning again in our land.

**Notes**

1  A term used by Ian Bradley in his book, *Colonies of Heaven*, DLT, 2000.

2  See Russ Parker, *Healing Wounded History*, SPCK, 2002.

3  H. B. Black, *Revival: Including the Prophetic Vision of Jean Darnall*, New Dawn, 1993.

4  See modernmonasticism@yahoogroups.com

5  H. Ellis, *Monasterium Briefing Notes*, August 2001. For a copy of the 'hub' model notes, email me at: Hughelli@aol.com

# 11. 'But — for Wales!'[1]

## JIM COTTER

There is an underlying strong sense of place at work throughout Jim Cotter's observations; how helpful is this given our nationalist tendencies on the one hand and the call to be a holy catholic church on the other? What is the connection between the particular and the universal?

Is it now time to press for some kind of quasi-Celtic pragmatism to inform the day-to-day Anglican rites and ceremonies?

*Jim Cotter taught at Lincoln Theological College before becoming Assistant Principal and then Course Director of the St Albans Ministerial Training Scheme. He is the author of a number of creative and original prayer books, most famously* Night Prayer. *He is now nurturing a small pilgrim place in Wales, called Eglwys Tecwyn Sant, Llandecwyn.*

Churches have a weighty past: it is not always the weight of glory. Echoes of past splendours still resonate, if faintly now, in the Church of England. Its clergy cling to honorifics, its bishops dress a little imperially, its cathedrals and larger parish churches proclaim a tiered order of society on the three levels of sanctuary, choir, and nave. Look for where there are carpets, cushions, and elaborate carvings, and you know which are the most important areas, fenced off to all but a few, the powerful snugly fitting into the picture of a powerful God. It was only in the late sixties that a rector and curate in Manchester did not know how to respond to the chief flower arranger as she clipped the stalks of her favourite chrysanthemums at the altar and said, 'It's such a wonderful privilege to be the only woman allowed in the sanctuary.'

> Come with me now over the border into the province of Wales, sister to Canterbury and York, and pay a visit to one or other of the many small churches, simple rectangles modelled on the long barns of the farms, at one time the only building suitable for public gatherings at the times of harvest and marriage, the rites of the passing of the seasons of the land and of human life. Most of these stone churches, built in medieval

times, often on ancient burial sites, sometimes rebuilt in the nineteenth century, have few if any memorials and inscriptions and little if any stained glass. There has rarely been enough money for those tablets to the wealthy (who are not thereby necessarily holy). The culture honours modest, untrumpeted contributions to poetry, music, prayer, and the common good. It is suspicious of titles that may claim too much in advance of evidence of continuing worth.

The contrast is, of course, unfair, not as clear-cut as those broad sketches might imply. There are many small, unpretentious churches in England and not a few examples of pomp and circumstance in Wales. You can find many a memorial to the English magistracy and the local colluding squirearchy in times gone by.

And that last remark may betray an unfair bias in the writer. But he remains uneasy not only at the thought of enthronements, but also when faced with attempts to be less formal in formal buildings, attempts that, in their language and choreography, lack the necessary gravitas of the surroundings. Informality is likely to be more suitable in small buildings. Of course there is a danger: too much informality can descend into sentimentality; intimacy is needed, but also dignity.

Since drafting this contribution, the writer has been listening to the latest recording by the Lindsays of Beethoven's last string quartet. Reference is made in the sleeve notes to 'Music in the Round', the festival of concerts hosted by the Lindsays each May in the Studio of the Crucible Theatre in Sheffield. These concerts, we are told, are 'famous for [their] informal, intimate, and intense atmosphere'. The rapt attention of the listeners at a typical concert is much more of an act of participation than is usual in the large concert hall, except perhaps from the Promenaders in the Royal Albert Hall.

The small and open space of the Crucible Theatre may point to parallels in the arrangements of small churches, but it is the three words 'informal, intimate, and intense' that particularly struck this writer. The tone of informality is set by the Lindsays themselves, who are usually dressed in open-necked shirts of four different colours but cut in the same style, neatly combining variety with unity – very Anglican! Large orchestras and choirs can look (and sound) impressive, but they do play at a distance and in, for some, culturally alienating dress. At the Studio the space itself – the seating stepped down and in the round – helps to establish an intimate atmosphere. The third word, 'intense', may not be quite as appropriate. 'Concentration' would have to be added, even the kind of awe that is near neighbour to wonder and love – rather than the awe that is nearer to fear and overwhelming power.

These opening sentiments give a clue to the reasons for an experiment being conducted at one of these churches in north-west Wales, a church that is tucked into the corner of Bae Ceredigion (Cardigan Bay), 600 feet above the estuary of the Afon Dwyryd, on whose opposite shore is the zany delight of Portmeirion, and a mile or so from the coast road between Porthmadog and Harlech. Eglwys Tecwyn Sant it is called, St Tecwyn's Church: church and enclosure, as well as parish, are known as Llandecwyn. The view of estuary and hills could be entered into a competition for the top ten views of Europe and expect at least the bronze.

The present building dates from 1879 and is a replacement for a medieval church that may well have been built around 1000 AD. Tecwyn himself came here in the 520s from the first monastic settlement on Ynys Enlli (Bardsey Island). We know nothing about him, except for his name and his presence. And that is typical of many of the dedications of churches in Wales: the saints are local and accessible and not exalted out of recognition into stained glass.

Generations of local families have been buried at Llandecwyn – to our knowledge it has been a burial place since at least 500 BC. It is therefore held in fierce affection by the local community, who feel honour-bound to continue, however infrequently, to worship in the church, and to pass it on to the next generation in good repair. Conventionally, the seats can be arranged in rows, facing lectern and altar, for the local

Diolchgarwch (harvest thanksgiving), Christmas carol service, and occasional baptism, marriage, or funeral. The design is simple, based on the traditional long barn, with a little Victorian influence in the height, the tiling, and the levels.

Of course, times have been a-changing. Congregations are fewer in number and older in age than they were, and regular parish worship is in another church a couple of miles away, at Llanfihangel-y-traethau (the church and enclosure of the archangel Michael by the seashores). But what a pity if Eglwys Tecwyn Sant were to be used only rarely, and closed on the other 360 days of the year.

So, in spring, summer, and autumn it is now open as a place for quiet prayer, simple hospitality, and thoughtful conversation – a small pilgrim place. By agreement with the parish and the diocese (Bangor), the church can have a somewhat different 'summer' look. Since all the furnishings are movable, they can be ordered either conventionally or in a rather different way – though always keeping the logic of the architecture that firmly places the altar-table against the east wall and resists any attempt to move it even a foot westwards. In summer, therefore, the simple (though heavy!) 'station-platform' benches can be re-arranged to make a more open, octagonal, space into which it is hoped that visitors feel easily invited. The space includes the small area which in larger churches would be choir and sanctuary: there is no 'fencing' of the altar-table – indeed, it forms one of the 'ends' of the octagon.

During each of the three summers of the project so far (this is being written at the beginning of October 2002), between 1,000 and 1,500 people have come to visit: some to tend graves or take part in a rite of passage; some as tourists, posses of passing walkers or carloads of view-seekers; some as pilgrims who have heard that something new is afoot. The challenge to those offering a welcome to visitors is gently to remove the cataracts from the glazed eyes of the tourist and to release the focused eyes of the pilgrim. Three 'rules' seem to help.

First, have one or two people on hand to welcome visitors – to invite rather than to intimidate! They may give a leaflet (Llandecwyn has a 'meditation trail' that takes you round the churchyard and the church, suggesting pauses and reflection) or say a few introductory words, and then slowly back away to allow people space and time to be, and after a while offer a cuppa (and maybe a listening ear) to those whose body language gives a clue to their needs.

Second, maintain a pattern of corporate prayer, at advertised times, simple in structure, lay-led in principle, lasting only fifteen to twenty minutes. It may comprise a short office of pilgrim prayer, a time of silence, and 'the prayer of solidarity' with human needs both local and wider, including by name those for whom prayer[2] has been asked. It may be that times of silence become the one uniting feature of all such 'small pilgrim places'.

Third, advertise, by leaflet, newspaper, and noticeboard, when the church will be open. Keep the hours regular, however few.

All this points to a modest vocation for anybody reading this who may by now be feeling a slight 'tug' from somewhere or other inside. Perhaps it is the vocation of the 'hospitaller', the term used in the Middle Ages for those who tended to the needs of pilgrims at stopping places on their journeys. The hospitaller needs to be confident and competent in a task pitched at a level akin to that of the Samaritan rather than the professional counsellor, of the St John Ambulance Brigade rather than the Royal College of Nursing. If this does stimulate that frisson of recognition in the reader, you are invited to get in touch with the name and address at the end of this chapter[3].

Let me go deeper. The 'Spirit-place' needs to be a 'breathing space'. Think of that ancient desire, articulated by Jesus of Nazareth in a moment of righteous anger, for a place of worship to be 'a house of prayer for all peoples'. Then think of some of the spaces 'set aside', those in universities and airports, perhaps also some small galleries and small gardens, as well as the very old small churches, chapels, and crypts, some dating from the early centuries of Christianity. They may be in the immediate care of one or other of the major religious traditions, or of one or other of the mainstream Christian denominations (or of a particular body of trustees: there is, for example, the Quiet Gardens Trust), but they may be trying to be hospitable to others who do not share all the emphases of their tradition.

Because there are pressures to make the best and frequent use of limited space, these 'set-aside' spaces tend to have few permanent objects in them. The symbols may be universal to humankind, the clutter may be kept at bay, and that which particular traditions use as part of their time of prayer, whether individual or corporate, may be stored in cupboards outside or at the back, and brought into focus as and when needed – and stored away again afterwards. After all, we are used to carrying in and out vessels and books and candles.

> What is at issue here is the balance. Are we being pressed to create more spaces that are empty because there is now a global need to discover how we human beings are united in the silence and emptiness of the Living One, in a mysticism that is waiting to be claimed by everybody and not only by the so-called spiritual élite? In the Tate Modern in London there is a room of paintings by Mark Rothko: it has the atmosphere of a chapel, and there are a few benches for visitors to sit in contemplation. It is a quiet room, 'informal, intimate, and intense'. And it is uncluttered. The single series of paintings speaks of a spare transcendence, gateways to the beyond. A small pilgrim place indeed.

If the carrying in and out of stuff, resisting the constant temptation to fill the space, sounds like hard work, so be it. We can hire consultants these days to help us clear dead wood from our homes: why not from our churches? Ask what still has life in it and what has been squeezed dry. Ask if the necessary spiritual discipline of remembrance can be done without the past dominating the future. This is difficult territory if it includes pews or flags, but the question is important. After all, a good architectural design is about the space created more than about the floor, walls, and roof. And even if vergers in cathedrals groan about moving the chairs for the umpteenth time in a week, a chairless nave can make a visitor gasp at the wonder of the empty space. Practically, that comes down to the chores– except that in a Christian understanding of chores it is more a matter of 'rising up' to them than of 'coming down'.

Of particular interest at Llandecwyn in the summer of 2002 was the request by the local Quakers for permission to assemble in the church for a Sunday meeting, and visits by the neighbouring Orthodox Tad (Father) Deiniol from Blaenau Ffestiniog with various guests, the one group drawn by the simplicity, the other by the foundation date, which was before the major divisions in the history of the Christian Church. Other groups have visited– branches of the Mothers' Union, diocesan clergy from across the border in the province of York, and parish weekends, as well as singles and couples seeking a breathing space.

There is something more to be said about the contrast between large and small. If you live in a rural area, you may make the occasional visit to a cathedral or a hypermarket– and make something of an occasion of it. But the everyday norm is likely to be on a smaller scale. If you travel around a lot you may well have noticed that the consumerist megachurch commonly known as Tesco is now opening small 'chapels' by the roadside: fuel for the car and fuel from the minimarket. It is the corner shop by another name– or franchise. And small post offices are now offering a greater variety of services to the local community, in neighbourhood, on housing estate, or in the village. Globalisation needs the multiplication of the small (there's always a small pilgrim place near you) as well as the concentration of the few. We need the cathedrals to remind us that we belong to something large and comprehensive, but the large building cannot be the frequent or regular place of worship for most people.

The tension between large and small can be expressed differently. It is the tension between the universal and the particular, expressed in churches, both symbols common to all and those unique to one particular church.

Because the octagonal praying space that has been created in Eglwys Tecwyn Sant is clear of clutter, four focal points stand out more clearly. They demonstrate the universal symbols of water (a bowl on a table, which can also be used as a font); air (the word carried on the breath from the sacred Scriptures, which at their heart have the struggle between 'God has chosen us for privilege, ourselves first and the rest damned' and 'God has chosen us to serve the good of all peoples, ourselves last, in by a narrow squeak); earth (a globe and a dish of sand for candles, for prayer for the world and for particular people); and fire (the altar of transfiguration and the table of oven-baked bread). Outside there is the water coming down as rain and streams, the air both windy and calm, the earth that is the sand of the beaches, the grass of the pastures, and the rocks of the mountains, and the fire that is the setting sun and the flash of lightning.

While in the cities a mere window box is a tenuous reminder of the source of our nourishment, and our mobility has weakened our sense of continuity with the past, all along the western coasts of these offshore islands of Europe there is still a valuing of the land (and think of Christianity's ambivalent record on the relationship of humankind to the rest of creation) and a valuing of the ancestors (the funeral is still the most important of social occasions), and, thank God, the communion of saints is very near, not least because we know nothing about most of them and so can better hope to be included. The 'valuing of presence' is almost palpable once you have taken time to listen to the *silence* – yet another universal which we both need and fear.

This respect for land and ancestors, for creation and history, comes from pre-Christian times, from the days of that 'primal vision' of which John V. Taylor wrote in an African context a generation ago, and which has parallels among the Aboriginal peoples of Australia, the Maori of Aotearoa/New Zealand, the Native American of Utah, Arizona, and New Mexico, to name but a few. A number of Welsh-speaking writers, among them Bobi Jones and Euros Bowen, are aware of these parallels. And this writer has been told that the All Blacks, when they visit these islands, enjoy their time in Wales most of all– not just because of the enthusi-asm for rugby, but because Maori and Cymry (the Welsh people) share a love of singing together and a deeper sense of community than is the current fashion in Lowland Britain. This sensibility about land and ancestors may have been given new depth and meaning by Christianity, but Christianity is the loser if it tries to obliterate it. The early peoples of any territory should be honoured, and such honouring includes the language, which in story, poetry, and music carries the 'ab-original' into contemporary heart and mind.

If you examine the Christian history of these islands, you become aware of the extent to which the Roman Catholic tradition has been influen-tial in the Republic of Ireland; the Presbyterian in Northern Ireland and Scotland; and the Anglican in England. In twenty-first century Wales none of these traditions is strong, perhaps because the Welsh have never taken to the centralising tendency of Rome, or the English establish-ment, easing now but dominant until disestablishment in 1920. The great chapels of Wales are also in decline, perhaps because the Welsh language is now encouraged by education and politics, perhaps also because nonconformity has on the whole lacked the sacramental sense that is palpable in the landscape here. That ancient sensibility is latent, hardly below the surface, and is finding expression in the renewal of some of the pilgrim sites, such as Pennant Melangell, tucked into a val-ley whose stream eventually makes its way into the River Severn, and Ynys Enlli itself, Bardsey Island, whence three pilgrimages in the Middle Ages were worth one to Rome. Wending their way down the Llyn Peninsula, via Clynnog Fawr and Pistyll and Llangwnnadl, come latter-day pilgrims, some footsore, others saddlesore, and some in the kind of comfort that Tecwyn and company would doubtless describe as wimp-ish. Something at once very old and very new is beginning to happen, something beyond denominational divisions, and in principle open to those who explore other paths into God.

Then think of that naked man on a cross, continuing disturber of naked power, of worldly power; in him this world is confronted by that 'other world', that other reality, that naked love, which interpenetrates the everyday. Think of religion's– and Jesus'– constant temptation to collude with or take over imperial power: ('All the kingdoms of this world I will give you...'). Perhaps the small pilgrim places can help us to be prised loose from these patterns, help us to pray and talk about power as enduring love, as wise governance, and as service to the common good. Maybe, by their very vulnerability, their very powerlessness, they may bring us again to the heart of it all, and to one another's hearts.

The Church in Wales has recently made a gift to those sister provinces on the other side of Offa's Dyke– and to the wider world– of a loved and respected archbishop, but that Church in Wales that is more comprehensive than merely its present Anglican form has yet other pearls of modest price to offer to the future of the Church of England.

**Notes**

[1] The title of this chapter is a quotation from Robert Bolt's play *A Man for All Seasons*. Sir Richard Rich has given false witness at Sir Thomas More's trial and been rewarded with the post of Attorney General for Wales. More comments: 'Why, Richard, it profits a man nothing to give his soul for the whole world, but for Wales.' In the context of the chapter the title is ironic and the intention is to redress the balance. Such a scurrilous remark has been typical of the English, though whether it was a quotation or an invention of the playwright, this writer does not know.

[2] An 'office book', with an order of prayer for each day of the week, with the title *Pilgrim Prayer*, is due to be published in the spring of 2003, as a bilingual book. It is compiled by Jim Cotter and has been translated into Welsh by Cynthia Davies.

[3] Please contact Jim Cotter, whose address is Dwylan, Stryd Fawr, Harlech, Gwynedd, LL46 2YA; jim@cottercairns.co.uk

# 12. Institutional and local change through church plants

## BOB AND MARY HOPKINS

Would it be legitimate practice to pay merely lip-service to those traditional 'orders' above us while, at the same time, seeking to make radical shifts in grassroots management of our churches?

Could we envisage a time when pomp, politicking, continuity with the past etc. became invisible - where the Church as we know it became a default mechanism in our spiritual journey, rather than an imperative?

*Bob and Mary Hopkins have been involved in church planting for many years, first based in St Helen's Merseyside, now based in Sheffield. Here they express how they believe the church planting movement has already begun to change the Church of England.*

Jesus told them still another parable: 'The kingdom of heaven is like yeast [leaven] that a woman took and mixed into a large amount of flour until it worked all through the dough' (Matthew 13:33 NIV).

Jesus likened the Kingdom of God to leaven. Leaven is not pure yeast, it is simply some of the previous day's dough with the active ingredient of yeast cells in it. Jesus' parable likens the Kingdom to the small amount of leaven/live dough put into a massive quantity (literally, 'three satas', that is, about twenty-two litres) of inert dough– with the power of explosive growth. The leaven kept on multiplying till it had spread through all the dough.

Acts 1:8 is Jesus' prophetic direction to the small number of disciples in Jerusalem that they would fulfil this Kingdom leavening of the world in expanding spheres of multiplication to the ends of the earth!

The narrative that follows through the chapters of Acts is structured to illustrate how this worked out in the practice of New Testament missionary church planting. As I have explained elsewhere[1], there was a rhythm of church planting, followed by concentration, and then further spreading out (Acts 9:31; 19:10). Both the detail and the three repeated summary verses in 6:7; 12:24 and 19:20 reinforce these repeated phases of increase and spread around the key mission sending cities of Jerusalem, Antioch and Ephesus. At the heart of this effective mission movement was the power of multiplication that Jesus alluded to in both parable and prophecy.

Some of the most effective mission in different parts of the world over the centuries since the New Testament has shown a similar pattern of focusing on a centre of strength or bridgehead, from which a movement of church planting has emanated. This may have been due to any one, or a combination of, factors, such as an effective contextual model of mission and church, a gifted and anointed leader(s) and/or openness of the culture or people group. Such fruitful Kingdom expansions have sometimes been referred to as people group movements.

## AN ANGLICAN CHURCH PLANTING MOVEMENT WITHOUT A MOVEMENT?

Over the past thirty years church planting has emerged in the Church of England as an intentional mission strategy. Initially in the early 1960s it was practised by a few radical pioneers[2]. Then what seemed like one or two per year through the 1970s became something like one per month through the 1980s and almost one per week in the early 1990s.

Accompanying this surge of mission activity has been a series of nine annual and then biannual national church planting conferences, starting in 1997. Numbers attending these conferences grew from sixty to seven hundred at their height.

All this is evidence of much ground having been broken and gives cause for real encouragement. There have been similar trends in other denominations and streams, leading some to talk of 'a modern church planting movement'. In the sense that it has gathered momentum and drawn many into it, it could be called a movement. But a movement of mission based on multiplying models of church it certainly is not.

To some extent, church planting has been victim of the UK church tendency to fads and fashions. So in the late 1990s the limelight shifted to other novelties. Fortunately, however, much of the early planting activity provoked the question 'What is church?' and so there emerged an emphasis on 'new ways of being church'. Our understanding is that these are just new ways to describe church planting. They embrace the conviction we have had from the start that we need lots of creative new sorts of church as well as (and often rather than) more churches[3].

George Lings, in his earlier chapter in this book, has helpfully described many of these new expressions of church that are being planted. These expand the scope and continue the momentum of the Church of England church planting movement– but there is still no clear evidence of a people group movement. They are a one by one process based on addition rather than multiplication. It is such a multiplying missionary movement that we have always looked for, prayed for and striven to see how to work for. Our hope is that such a movement could not only transform the Church of England, but our nation.

## THE BARRIERS AND HINDRANCES

We would recognise that some of the greatest barriers to such a multiplying movement are not just institutional, but are in our minds and hearts. We have rigid concepts and expectations of church as we have known it. We also shrink from the challenges and sacrifices involved in laying down our lives so that others might come to know the love of Jesus.

Also, we don't have the expectation or practice that supports my conviction that the church is a 'Jesus community of disciple-making disciples[4]. We don't function as such self-reproducing units either as individual followers of Jesus, or in how we do small groups or larger gatherings.

Then, of course, there are the structural barriers of the parish system and clerical hierarchies, as well as a system of leadership selection, training and deployment that is geared for maintaining the existing patterns.

## NEW GROUND DEFINITELY BROKEN

The area in which there has been most movement has been the attitude of the Church of England to church planting and mission. Whereas at the end of the 1980s many national leaders were uncertain whether church planting was Anglican at all, now at least in most quarters it is recognised and affirmed. Church planting and mission are spoken of positively as essentials for the way ahead, even if we are less certain how to bring them about.

The biggest step here was probably the work of the bishops' working group on church planting that in 1994 produced the report *Breaking New Ground*. Unanimously approved by the House of Bishops and commended by General Synod, it has gradually helped to bring about a transformed climate of thinking.

One of the most significant conclusions of *Breaking New Ground* comes in the first chapter. This is the recognition that the Church of England in its current social and cultural context can no longer rely on the single understanding of ministry and mission expressed in the territorial reality of the parish. Rather, developments in how people now live out their lives mean that there are three overlapping realities:

1. territory– the territory of the parish;
2. geographical neighbourhoods, which may no longer bear any relation to parishes and may overlap several parishes;
3. networks of relationship that are not geographically based and therefore bear no relation either to neighbourhoods where people live (or at least sleep) or to a territorial legal entity of the parish. The report recognises the increasing importance of these networks.

Some have suggested that this is the most radical conclusion of the *Breaking New Ground*. Nowhere, however, is there any serious addressing of the implications of this radical analysis for the future of the Church of England.

The parish system based on territory remains the predominant way in which the Church of England continues to do church, and all its structures and legal formulations are formed around the concept. Hence the recognition of the three realities raises the most fundamental questions. So far-reaching are the implications that it is perhaps not surprising that the first Breaking New Ground report did not take on this challenge. It merely settled for a descriptive analysis of the sorts of church planting that were happening a decade ago and focused on a proposal that these early experiments be encouraged within the existing frameworks.

## THE USE OF PRECEDENT TO TRY TO ACCOMMODATE MORE RADICAL CHURCH PLANTING INITIATIVES

Over the past ten years the number of church plants has continued to increase and their range to diversify. Both George Lings and Martin Cavender have referred to the English instinct for using precedent, rather than the creation of new structures or new laws, as a way of validating innovations. Bearing in mind the length of time that it takes to frame and pass new law in the Church of England, there is also a pragmatic benefit in this line of approach. The application of this principle has led to the following main ways forward:

### 1. Use of the conventional district

Where a church plant has focused on a neighbourhood with real geographic identity (such as a new housing estate) then the device of a conventional district has been used with significant success. One of the great advantages of this constitutional device is that it can be set up extremely quickly with the agreement of the incumbents of all the parishes affected by the new neighbourhood reality. Its great weakness is that its continuance depends on the agreement of all participating incumbents, who may change. A secondary disadvantage that the new church plant as it thrives has no real sense of existence in parity to the other parish churches in the deanery and the diocese. However, the nature of such geographic plants into discrete neighbourhoods means that if they succeed, they may well fit within the historic parish concept and in time this may lead to their being recognised as parishes in their own right.

The use of this precedent therefore seems not too ill suited to the realities of this pattern of mission and ministry. At least the sort of church that is created still relates to a geographic entity and it is merely that a corresponding new geographic legal and territorial entity has to be created at some stage. The two-step potential from conventional district in the early pioneer phases through to forming a full parish can be quite a satisfactory process and there are examples where this has successfully occurred.

### 2. The Extra Parochial Place (EPP)

This is a precedent that has been helpfully used in a number of church plants that do not relate to a particular territory or neighbourhood. Again, I think it was George Lings and Martin Cavender who, in reviewing the situation for the Carpenters Arms plant in Deal, came up with this precedent and over a period of several years managed to work it through to the Privy Council[5].

The EPP was originally created as a structural and legal entity to cover such non-parish ministry as schools, colleges and military service chaplaincies. The fact that they do not have a parish basis but rather are framed according to the place where the gathered community meets, has made this device a possibility for church planting mission projects that are focused on non- geographic social networks. The fact that once set up, the place of meeting specified can be changed relatively easily is also a positive feature that enables growth and change.

On the down side, is the fact already referred to that the process is long and has to go to the Privy Council for ratification. They also require ratification of the incumbent of the parish in which it meets. Furthermore, as a number of other church plants that have sought to follow the Deal precedent have found, the road can be quite difficult. The highly successful Springfield church plant in Wallington's, Carshalton, had their application for EPP status rejected initially. Several years later, with a change in diocesan personnel, the attitude was reversed and now, some seven years on, Springfield is achieving EPP status.

### 3. Reliance on a purely relational rather than structural or legal framework

In the case of 'The Net' in Huddersfield, the Archdeacon, having explored the possibilities of EPP, has taken the line that he thinks grace rather than law should prevail in such new ways of doing church. He has therefore piloted the development through on the basis of his relationship with the leader of the plant, David Male, and others in the diocese. The basis and understanding on which the church plant has gone ahead has been committed to paper but this does not have any legal weight within the existing statues of the Church of England. Harvest NAC in the Canterbury Diocese would be another example of an experimental non-parish church plant that has progressed well on this basis.

George Lings has referred to this approach as 'having friends in high places' or 'an advocate at court' [6]. In its call to grace rather than law, this approach seems, at first sight, very attractive. But not only is it extremely vulnerable to a change of personnel (as has been shown from experiences all over the country), this does not seem a satisfactory way for the church to manage the way forward in response to one of the biggest challenges for mission today– the fact that social and cultural networks are becoming the predominant way in which people live their lives.

## THE NEED FOR MORE RADICAL RECOGNITION
## OF THE TRUE CULTURAL REALITY FOR MISSION

We now come to what seems to us to be the fulcrum and turning point in our reflections. In much of our thinking over the past years, we have taken as our starting point the Church as it is and the mission examples as they have sought to develop within the existing structure and legal framework. I think it is time for me to follow my own dictum, namely, that we need to 'stop starting with the Church'. If our thinking begins and is shaped by the Church as it is, and is only stretched by the faltering steps at new ways of doing church made possible within the existing structures, then we may never see the true shape in which things need to develop.

Stepping back and seeing the big picture involves taking as our starting point the cultural context for mission. A detailed analysis of Western postmodern culture reveals a wide range of overlapping, connected networks. All sorts of factors– music, entertainment, sport, fashion, hobby, career– provide the interconnecting fabric that link together some smaller and some larger non-geographic networks or sub-cultures. It seems to me that when seeking to determine the appropriate mission response of the Church a crucial key is the recognition of this connectedness between the different socio-cultural subsets of our society.

## LESSONS FROM MOVEMENTS
## OF MISSION AND CHURCH PLANTING

To return to the importance of learning from history and the wider global Church, we referred earlier to the power and effectiveness of church planting movements for mission. Over the last few centuries, some of the most important and exciting missionary developments have been when the gospel has effectively engaged with a particular culture or subculture and the pattern of church multiplication has enabled a movement to spread throughout that context. As Western culture has moved from Christendom to post-Christendom and now, in great swathes, to pre-Christian, we have held a passionate hope and prayer that God would release such movements of mission within our own nation. If the observation in our previous section is correct that despite the diversity of our culture there is a connectedness of different sub-cultural sets, then the potential is surely there for a whole range of missionary movements of church planting.

## HOW DO YOU ORDER
## MULTIPLICATION AND A MOVEMENT?

Once we take seriously the existence of post-Christendom and pre-Christian connected networks and the possibility that multiplying movements of church planting would be the most effective mission response, we beg the question: How are we to order such a multiplying movement? If we open up our minds to this sort of mission possibility in the UK, then it seems to me conclusive that there is no way that this can be accommodated within the existing parish-based structures and legal frameworks. So long as we have a one by one approach, then one or even two church plants can relate back to a mother parish church congregation. They may well, as George Lings and others have observed, lack a lot of strength and vitality as a result of being robbed of the 'three-self' characteristics, but they may be able to get some degree of accountability, oversight, encouragement and training from a mother parish congregation that takes the exceptional step of gearing itself up to resource one or two congregations other than itself.

Our ecclesiology, however, leads us to believe that order is essential for the healthy development of life. We are left, therefore, with the question: If we are going to have missionary movements in the many network subcultures of postmodernism, how are we going to *order* such movements? For their healthy development and continuing effective mission, it will be essential that they remain connected and have appropriate patterns and structures for accountability, oversight, encouragement, training, etc. There seems no way that these patterns and structures can be adequately provided by seeking to drip feed or in some way bolt new expressions of church on to existing diocesan provision, geared as it is to a whole diversity of parish needs. A form of ordering is needed that has something of the character and quality of the subculture concerned.

The early pioneer models of non-parish, non-geographic network church plants seem to bear out these challenging conclusions. By continuing with the parish as the dominant and defining identity of our Church to which all new expressions of church have to find relationship, we end up with initiatives like Tommy's in Nottingham, The Net in Huddersfield and B1 in Birmingham, which are separate islands relating in a one off exceptional structure to their diocese.

## THE ONLY CONCLUSION SEEMS TO BE THAT WE MUST HAVE A PARALLEL ORDER/STRUCTURE

As soon as *Breaking New Ground 1* had recognised the substantial and increasing reality of non-geographic social networks, it had begged the question as to what new structure would be required to provide an order to support and encourage effective mission and church planting in such networks. This can now be seen all too clearly. If we are not to be limited to isolated patches of growth and encouragement we have to break out and see movements of mission.

If we are to return to the vision that Jesus gave of leaven that multiplies and spreads, we shall need to work with strong centres and intentionally mobilise out from them. Rather than being threatened by the large growing churches, we need a positive view of their potential as 'minsters', or resource churches. The Sheffield Diocese has boldly taken initial steps here[7]. Such large churches need to accept the challenge of going beyond merely setting targets for their own growth. Rather, accepting the mission imperative, they should train and give away of their best. But this giving away must not to be in ones and twos to struggling, declining situations where those who go will be swamped, but in strength, to situations where a missionary agenda can be set and culturally appropriate evangelism and growth pursued. The Wakefield Diocese have gone half-way toward this goal with their innovation of 'turn-around teams'. But again it is one by one and without the vision or authority for multiplication.

Again we come back to the nagging question: How will such new patterns be ordered to set them free to flow? There is an urgent need to foresee and prepare for new structures that will support and encourage culturally related movements of church planting. This should not just be reactively and reluctantly reorganising to cope with the exceptional mission movement as it emerges here or there. So let's be bold and seek to answer our own question!

### 1. Mission orders
First, we need to re-invent twenty-first century missionary orders. These would allow minster churches to identify, train and release bands of missional leaders to pioneer movements of new expressions of church. The Sheffield Diocese is exploring this with St Thomas' Church. St Thomas' has grown from four congregations meeting in the parish church in the early 1990s to some twenty clusters (missionary congregations) engaging all sorts of contexts and sub-cultures across the city. They have also developed a leadership training programme called 'Tribal Training' that has multiplied to seven centres around the UK and Ireland, and had some 150 participants in 2001.

## 2. Parallel network deaneries/dioceses

The missional congregations and new expressions for church planted by the leaders in such mission orders will not themselves be religious orders. They will need to be connected and in accountable relationships in the same way as existing local parish churches. Hence, the second thing we need is a parallel, overlapping structure, something as bold as a network deanery and a network diocese, to hold together the movement of new communities of faith.

Such a formulation and structure will relate the movement of multiplying churches to one another. It will recognise the clear flow of authority and anointing from the leaders and will also root them clearly within the Anglican family and accountability. To be consistent with the geographic parish, such networks should be challenged to define their socio-cultural mission focus, thereby also giving them an overlapping 'cure of souls'.

Such new structures are not only needed for the increasing social reality of network subcultures. There are other situations where they will release mission multiplication and movement in new ways. In particular, they are needed in areas of our country where *neighbourhood* is still the predominant social reality– the urban priority estates of our northern cities. An emerging example here would be the resource centre of the World Wide Message Tribe, so effective in mission into Manchester schools. This has been followed by multiplying teams of young adults moving in, in strength, to the neediest estates. These teams have seen radical transformation, including tumbling crime figures, that have caught police and government attention[8]. But so far the emerging new expressions of church are bolted on, one by one, to existing local congregations. It is my conviction that the cultural gap is far too wide for this to work, and that re-ordering with a mission order and a movement of connected missional communities would be more appropriate and would release more momentum.

Such radical new structuring could come surprisingly easily and encompass unexpected forms, such as parishes embracing the same mission model.
I could also foresee a network deanery of parishes within a diocese seriously adopting cell church. Here a measure of authority and anointing will flow

from the network area dean who heads up a minster church that leads the way and resources the movement of cells through the linked, but not necessarily geographically related, parishes.

These proposals shake the existing foundations. They challenge patterns of control and power bases. But are we going to take seriously our own words about the priority of mission and proactively plan for mission enabling structures? A diocese here or there is taking tentative steps, but can we look to bold national leadership to press forward on a broad front? It is encouraging that Archbishop Rowan Williams was the first to recognise two modern mission orders in his Monmouth Diocese and led the way on a long-discussed permanent diaconate. He also introduced the idea of 'a mixed economy in mission'[9] in the report on the future of the Church in Wales. We pray for him and for many more radical new mission motivated initiatives, initiatives radical enough to meet the challenge of a dire situation.

## REALLY RADICAL ACTION MATCHING RADICAL TALK

Archbishop Rowan's lead in introducing the concept of a mixed economy in Wales has not been just words. It is beginning to work out in a national policy in Wales with the aim of maintaining commitment to existing traditional parish forms of worship and ministry but encouraging everyone to think of planting parallel new missionary communities of faith. Money and action is beginning to back this up. In Merthyr Tidfill, a series of pub-based Alpha courses have led to converts from non-churched backgrounds. They have been drawn in through a network of family, friends and workmates that spreads beyond the parish, across deaneries and even into the next diocese. When it was clear that most were not going to be drawn into the existing parish worship, the Bishop of Llandaff funded a church planter with the authority to do 'whatever it takes to church them, ignoring all existing Church in Wales policy'.

We wonder whether it is significant that the radical mission initiatives in Monmouth flowed from an early move by the then Bishop Rowan to disband the committee responsible for mission, the 'Council for Witness'. We gather that a couple of years later a new forum was constituted to brainstorm ideas twice a year, but with strong visionary leadership continuing.

This highlights the real crunch issue. Can our national leaders gain the power to introduce radical structural change? The institutions' ability to resist change is the main hindrance to change in the Church. Radical new mission initiatives can come from the grassroots but radical enabling structural change can only come from the top. The problem here is that the more democratised an institution the less able it is to implement the costly change that is needed in order to invest for the long term future. Rather, all the forces conspire to protect and preserve the interests of every existing group.

Here two developments seem most significant. Firstly, attempts to introduce more radical executive power at the top through Turnbull have resulted in an Archbishops' Council that is little more than an agenda sifting body for Synod, which has lost none of its powers to block, delay or amend any radical proposal for change.

Secondly, it is significant that in Bishop Nazir-Ali's book[10] on the future of the Church of England, he takes as his ideal model, the North African church structure in the early centuries, a democratised system that led to the extinction of that Church when faced with radical change (precisely and chillingly illustrating, I believe, the self-preservation paralysis of synods!).

So what would be a rational response to this argument? Yes, we need to pray for lots more 'radical Wesleys' to pioneer effective mission models that lead to grassroots movements. But if we are not to lose them again, we need equally radical change at the top. Why not something like this . . .

I propose a decade of experimentation in mission and structure. Disband General Synod and diocesan synods for ten years (five if we are white with fear at the prospect). Allow archbishops (perhaps with their councils) and bishops to lead in mission. Such experiment would involve establishing provisional new enabling powers that could be reviewed at the end of the period. The saving of millions of pounds on synodical processes would provide good pump priming for mission. I suggest, however, that this would be nothing compared to the significance of releasing missional leadership. Of course, in the decade we might need to make sure we appointed a whole different sort of missional leader as bishops. They, like Archbishop Rowan, would understand that strong directive leadership in times of rapid change and challenge to the Church, is in fact the appropriate model of servant leadership.

**Notes**

[1]  Bob Hopkins, *Church Planting*, Grove Evangelism Series No. 4, 1988, pp. 11-12, and Bob Hopkins and Richard White, *Enabling Church Planting*, CPAS, 1995, p. 5.

[2]  See Eddie Gibbs, Ten Growing Churches, MARC, 1984, ch. 7, and Ted Longman, *The Church on the Estate*, CPAS Fellowship Paper 282-283, 1973.

[3]  Bob Hopkins (ed.), *Planting New Churches*, Eagle, 1991, pp. 15, 124.

[4]  Michael Green (ed.), *Church Without Walls*, Paternoster, 2002, p. 43.

[5]  G. Lings, *New Ground in Church Planting*, Grove Evangelism No. 27, 1994, p.8.

[6]  G. Lings, 'New Canterbury Tales', in *Encounters on the Edge* No. 7, The Sheffield Centre, 2000.

[7]  Sheffield Diocesan Strategy Report, 1999-2004, Section 2.49 to 2.51, also Recommendation 9.

[8]  George Lings, *Encounters on the Edge* No. 14, The Sheffield Centre, 2002.

[9]  *Good News in Wales*, Church in Wales, 1999.

[10] Bishop Nazir-Ali, *Shapes of the Church to Come*, Kingsway, 2001.

# 13. Disestablishment – the straightforward case[1]

## COLIN BUCHANAN

Is it necessary for the Church of England to become disestablished in order for it to recover its integrity?

*Colin Buchanan is the Bishop of Woolwich and was previously the Bishop of Aston, and Principal of St John's College, Nottingham. He is well known as a campaigner for disestablishment.*

If you want to understand the Reformation in two or three lines, then you need to visualise yourselves running a West African developing nation, where, as you look around, you find that a major transnational, say, the Coca-Cola Company, is in fact in a prime position in your land. It is siphoning off its profits to New York and it has thousands of servants among your citizens, each of whom owes a higher allegiance to New York than to your (and their) country. Well, as the leader of a self-respecting West African nation you take one obvious step– you expropriate. That was Henry VIII's part in the Reformation. He expropriated the local branch in England of a great transnational religious (but also commercial) company, the headquarters of which were in Rome; and he achieved this by severing the management's connection with Rome. He ruled that every bishop and clergyman had to swear loyalty to the King as supreme head on earth of the Church of England and in certain situations disavow any loyalty to the Pope. That was Henry VIII's remedy. To this day the diocesan bishops of the Church of England are appointed under Henry VIII's legislation of 1534, legislation that ensured that bishops acknowledged that they got their authority solely from him and owed their loyalty solely to him.

Now our supposed West African nation first of all changes the management. But that has not yet made any difference to the product on sale at the corner shop. The Coca-Cola recipe and the actual drink both remain exactly the same. And so it was in Henry's reign– the worship at the parish church was unaffected by the change (it was only that the nation now had power to change the recipe if it seemed good to them to do so). The power, certainly, was there and change duly happened. In Edward VI's reign, the local management altered the recipe. From the point of view of Rome, the Church of England was not now simply improperly in schism: it had also put itself into terrible heresy. This reminds me that I was once in Peru, where an old student of mine was bishop, and the locals told me that they had in fact dispossessed Coca-Cola out there, and had produced some stuff of their own called Inca-Cola. Someone sent it to a laboratory for analysis and a fortnight later they had got back a letter saying, 'We are grieved to report that your horse has hepatitis.'

In the illustration I'm offering you, however, the local recipe was a vast improvement on the one that had been abandoned. Henry VIII had retained Latin services identical with those of the Pope. The only thing was, you prayed against the Pope, instead of for him. But now Edward VI, with Cranmer, of course, at the helm, put through a total, radical reformation of the worship of the Church and, indeed, of the doctrinal articles. Although there were hiccups in Mary's reign, and again in the Commonwealth, and in James II's reign, that State Protestantism introduced by Edward VI was the principal characteristic of religion in England through the sixteenth and seventeenth centuries. The nation of England now had a religious monopoly run by the State; the Church of England was really a department of State. The history of the 450 years to the present day can be seen as a period of five distinctly articulated separate phases in what is now called the establishment[2].

The first phase runs from Cranmer's time to 1689 and in it you have a State monopoly of religious practice. All forms of belief and worship are imposed centrally, and imposed on everyone– that is what an 'Act of Uniformity' means. Everyone is to conform. If they will not conform, they will be severely penalised. As a result, some go to prison, others are prohibited from meeting to pray, and so on. That is the State monopoly period. Church and State are a single, almost monolithic, entity, and the government of the citizens of the State very naturally govern the same people in their other capacity as members of the Church.

The second phase comes after 1689, when the dissenters, having actually helped the Church of England to see off James II and have him replaced, are entitled to some sympathetic treatment. This is the period of State privilege for the Church of England, and toleration of other groupings. It is still pretty uncomfortable to be a Roman Catholic, but if you are a dissenter, life is much better after 1689. Nevertheless, technically you still have to belong to the Church of England before you can hold a variety of posts, including office under the Crown. All the privilege is with the Church of England. But the Church is still run by Parliament, and indeed early in the eighteenth century the Convocations of the clergy ceased to meet[3]. This second period, the period of privilege, ran to 1830.

The third phase is ushered in with the Reform Parliament. The enfranchising of Roman Catholics from 1830 and the composition of the resulting Parliaments means that for the first time Parliament is not visibly and overtly Anglican. Almost immediately that reformed Parliament passes a law uniting Irish bishoprics. Now these need uniting. Some of the Southern bishoprics in Ireland have very few worshippers but enormous benefice income for rather over-stocked livings and bishoprics[4]. Uniting them is a sensible thing to do, but it is done by naked parliamentary power without so much as a by-your-leave from the Church, who are not consulted.

To be fair, as we have seen above, there isn't much of a Church of England (actually in those days a 'United Church of England and Ireland') to consult. The Church does not have an identifiable set of governing organs separate from those of the State. The State governing bodies are the Church's governing bodies. But in 1833, John Keble in his Assize Sermon, and John Henry Newman in the *Tracts for the Times*, start to attack this Irish bishoprics legislation as stemming from the wicked hands of Erastianism, and executed by a Parliament that, though not committed to a theological basis, is nevertheless laying organising hands upon the life of the Church.

Thus my third phase, from 1830 (or perhaps 1833) onwards until 1920, is the period when bishops, clergy and worshippers are struggling to find an identify for the Church of England separate from that of the State. And so in that time you get the restoration of the Convocations, the creation of the house of lay people (lay men, of course), and also in 1870 the disestablishment of the Church of Ireland[5]. The disestablishment of the Church in Wales follows, finally being put through in 1920. During these ninety years the Anglo-Catholic movement resists every attempt of the State to bring their clergy into line. They refuse to recognise the court judgments; some clergy go to jail rather than obey secular courts; and they denounce State power over the Church of England. Of course, that protest goes right back to the Assize Sermon and to the *Tracts*, with the protagonists staking their authority upon the 'apostolic succession' and not upon the mere historical accident of a State connection. This latter is now played down and secular courts are not recognised as having jurisdiction in spiritual matters. And, of course, this causes terrible rumpuses in Parliament, which finally lead to the next stage.

The fourth phase runs from 1920 onwards, when the Church Assembly is set up and when the preparation of legislation for the Church of England is distanced a whisker or more from State processes because it is now prepared in the Church Assembly and only goes to Parliament for what in effect are third readings, without Parliament having power of amendment in either House. And yet immediately that procedure is in place, a crisis occurs that brings it deeply into question. In December 927 the proposed Prayer Book, having gone through the Church Assembly and having been passed on to Parliament (simply for that yes-or-no vote), is then rejected by the Commons. The *Hansard* of that debate makes wonderful reading – the House of Commons is considering whether the Church of England is moving towards Rome. The members vote the book out by 238 votes to 205; and six months later give the same treatment to a marginally re-touched book, with which the Church Assembly are trying a second throw, this time defeating it by 266 votes to 220, if after a less colourful debate.

The House of Bishops views the double defeat by Parliament as a major crisis. They resolve never to take liturgy to Parliament again, and vow that they must get powers to create and authorise liturgy themselves. Thus begins the process of devolving powers from Parliament to what is now the General Synod, so that, nearly fifty years on from 1928, under the Worship and

Doctrine Measure, the Church of England again has powers over liturgy; and similarly, again by devolution from Parliament, it has powers to create new dioceses, to organise the union and changing of parishes, and to take a host of other decisions about its own life.

But not everything is so devolved, and when the ordination of women comes up in 1992, General Synod puts it through by a tight two-thirds vote, and then there is a year's delay before Parliament considers it. And if in 1992 there had been a hung Parliament– remember, John Major just scraped in– the Ecclesiastical Committee might never have been appointed (this is the body which receives and considers Measures from the Synod before they go to Parliament) before another General Election– resulting in another wasted year– and the legislation for the ordination of women would have taken two years in all from being passed in Synod. We are absolutely dependent not just upon parliamentary approval but even upon the parliamentary timetable: a quite astonishing captivity.

But I am running ahead. My fifth period begins in 1970. The old Church Assembly time runs out in 1970 with the formation of the General Synod. That coincides with the report of the Chadwick Commission, *Church and State 1970*, the last report on Church and State relationships there has been (which, at the time of writing, means that a thirty-three-year period has passed without a commission or working party addressing this pressing issue[6]). And, having got a Church identity separate from that of the State, which is clearly what the standing of the Church Assembly produced, and what the House of Bishops' Statement after 1928 was, in the last analysis, asserting, the Church has now the power to create liturgy without reference to what is, in effect, the secular arm.

Here then is the ideological split– on the one hand, a nation, a State, the sum of all its citizens, and on the other hand, an identifiable, smaller, body within the State, a confessional Christian body, the Church of England. No one can now pretend that the two entities are one. Yet the creation of a separate identity for the Church involves a split that Henry VIII would never have allowed. The creation of electoral rolls and PCCs in 1920 gave substance to that separable identity, and, as it has grown, so the idea that somehow the whole country is Christian, that the whole nation is Anglican by decree, has become more and more incredible.

If the period of 1920-1970, my fourth phase, included some struggling about separate identities, there is little room for doubt that my fifth phase, the post-1970 era, is the era of total incredibility about the establishment. I submit that you have to live by fantasy to believe in the Church of England's establishment on the Henrician basis that State and Church are one. No, there now has to be a totally different rationale, it has to be about the relationship between two separate entities; and, on my analysis, that relationship is in fact one of the captivity of the Church of England to the secular State *apparatus*. It is the captivity of a goat on a very long chain. The goat can browse and graze freely much of the time, and can even persuade itself that it is totally free– but on occasion (and I am about to come to those occasions) it pulls against the stake at the limit of its long chain, and then it finds itself captive.

So, what is the establishment? On a cool analysis it is simply the existence of laws of any sort that separately touch our particular Church. That's the nearest definition the Church and State Commissions have come to. If a religious body is governed by the same laws as any other religious body, or as a charitable voluntary body would be, then it is not established. If there are laws in Parliament that specifically identify us and say things to or about us, then we are established. That is, I hope, an unemotive way of addressing the matter. It does, perhaps, leave open an interesting question in relation to the Church of Scotland, which has freedom to run itself, and I want to say it is not an established Church. Though it claims to be a 'national' Church, it is in fact a Church by law disestablished. In other words, the last parliamentary law to apply to the Church of Scotland was that which set it free, just as the last law to apply to an African colony or to the dominion of Canada in the North American Act is the one that actually says, 'From now on you'll get no more legislation from us and this winds up all legislation from us.' But the Church of England has still got a whole series of laws that give us this distinct established position, and I must therefore touch upon the particular issues that affect us.

Parliament has now, remember, no religious tests. In fact, you could not, I think, be a Parliamentarian as an atheist in the 1830s, and it was Charles Bradlaugh, was it not, much later in that century, who fought the battles about God, so that you do not now have to take an oath before God to be a member of the Commons. There are no religious tests, and Parliament is sovereign. And therefore, whatever a bishop may write to the Press, as happens sometimes, there is actually no formal place of appeal in Christian theology to touch the life of this nation. You cannot, for instance, if you are debating abortion, do other than simply go with the views of the majority or the views the majority thinks they will get away with, with their constituents or with their party manifesto. You have no sanctions at all that can be expressed by saying, 'But we're Christians'– for the members of the Commons are not there as Christians. Some may, of course, have a Christian faith, but you get them there by a totally random process. It is sheer chance who got elected in this or that constituency, and in this one a Christian was standing, but he was on the losing side, and in that one, one was standing and he was on the winning side, because of the way the votes went *for other reasons*. It is impossible to come into the Commons and say you've been chartered as a Christian to stand for anything. Oh, they still have prayers and a certain amount of, as it were, run-on ceremonial, but in the last analysis the sovereignty of this country is exercised by a body with no religious tests or affiliation built into its naturel. The Church of England has no necessary leverage upon decisions of the Commons. But, conversely, laws stand in place whereby parliamentary unbelievers, as for political purposes they must be regarded, govern the believers of the Church of England. And that, I put it to you, is Erastianism.

So what are those points where the chain stretches tight, and the captivity is clear?

I suppose that first in people's minds at the moment is the appointment of diocesan bishops. Diocesan bishops are appointed in the following way. A bishop dies. By Henry VIII's law of 1534 the monarch chooses someone else, and writes to the dean and chapter of the cathedral of the vacant diocese saying, 'Because Brother Ambrose has died and you're without the solace of a chief pastor, you are to meet and choose the man whose name I now forward to you.' The man's name has already been announced to the Press, and the election is a deceit. The dean and chapter then elect, and, at an extraordinary ceremony called the Confirmation, church lawyers get together with Her Majesty's nominee, and it is proved he really is the man elected. He is then confirmed by lawyers and becomes at that moment the Bishop of Puddlecaster. If not yet a bishop, he is consecrated. He pays homage, swearing that he gets all his authority, spiritual as well as temporal, from Her Majesty alone[7]. Then he can be enthroned.

In recent years the law has remained unchanged, but we have put a whole series of conventions into the process. For more than a century, the Prime Minister, as chief adviser to the Crown, has in fact given the name to the monarch. In the 1960s we gained vacancy in see committees, which the Prime Minister's appointments secretary would consult. Then in the late 1970s came the Crown Appointments Commission. This arose from the Church and State Report in 1970 (the Chadwick Report) that had led to the General Synod in 1974 saying that the decisive voice in the appointment of bishops should lie with the Church[8].

When Donald Coggan and Norman Anderson went to see first of all Harold Wilson and then Jim Callaghan, these Prime Ministers wouldn't allow 'the decisive voice' to the Church. They said that, because the diocesan bishops go on to the House of Lords, they are in effect a political appointment, and the prime minister of the day must have at the very least a choice between two names to exercise. So the Crown Appointments Commission, which has two archbishops, three elected clergy from General Synod, three elected laity from General Synod and four representatives from the vacant diocese, meets together for twenty-four hours and finds two names to send to Downing Street, and the PM then picks one (not necessarily the one favoured by the Commission)– and may do so for arbitrary or personal or political reasons. He is not accountable for his choice.

We need an open, transparent and participatory church method of appointing bishops in which, when they come into their diocese, they know they are wanted. At best, at the moment they know that four people may have put them second on their list[9]. That's all. Bishops come in, as it were, by dint of secular force majeure, not of popular call within the life of the body spiritual.

But Parliament itself has a reform coming up. The House of Lords is overdue to change. The place of bishops is bound to change, and the Callaghan argument (still current) that prime ministers must have a discretion as between two names, on the grounds they are going to the Lords, will then be superseded by events. And if there is to be Church of England representation in a Second Chamber, then we need to appoint those representatives ourselves (as any other section of society with representation would do).

The second major constricting feature of the present establishment is the control of legislation by Parliament. Yes, much Parliamentary legislation has devolved powers to the General Synod. But many things are not devolved, and, for instance, the ordination of women, and perhaps even women as bishops, cannot happen without legislation going through Parliament, where not only do the members of English constituencies look pretty puzzled by theological questions, but in fact the Welsh, Scottish and Northern Irish MPs also vote on our future. It is a most absurd, wildly unbelievable system, and it is my conviction that we ought ourselves to produce the measure to end all measures, to draft the disestablishing legislation in Synod and send it to Parliament.

Next is the monarchy. Prince Charles went on record a while back saying he did not see why a Roman Catholic cannot be monarch in this country. But the monarch is the one person who by law must be C of E, and I do not see how the Pope can allow dual membership at that point, for the monarch is the supreme governor of the Church of England as things are, and in that capacity, in fact, signs canon law, appoints diocesan bishops, and as a matter of fact more or less convenes General Synod. And, of course, the historic understanding is that the monarch is at Communion at his or her coronation.

Establishment issues run down into parish life also– the historic right in law to marry (once anyway) in the parish church; the right of parishioners of any faith or none to participate in the annual choice of churchwardens; the special Faculty jurisdiction which puts Church of England places of worship into a distinct separate category for planning and alteration purposes. Some of these arcane features still suggest the Tudor notion that the citizens of England are the Church of England[10]. But the major limitations arise at national level in connection with rules constrained by Parliament, and appointments in the hands of Downing Street.

So how would we better off without these constraints? Wouldl striking off the shackles bring growth – or spiritual revival? Here I have to tread carefully. Suppose a PCC were to say, 'What good will repairing the roof (or cleaning the drains do)? Will taking such trouble really fill the church?' The answer cannot be a straight 'yes', for there is no such heavenly prospectus. But reversing the question soon brings home the truth. If we do not repair the roof or do not clean the drains, can healthy congregational life with promise of growth go on? And the answer to that has to be, 'No, or at least not in the middle- or long-term.' To groan under the present constraints ought to be enough to convince the leaders of the Church of England that we should be free, irrespective of other consequences; and Anglicans ought to be embarrassed to have privileges denied to other denominations. So in one sense I urge disestablishment simply because it is right in itself– we simply ought not to belong to the State *apparatus* at the places we do and in the ways we do. Thus we should seek our freedom without undue calculation of benefits – the freedom is right in itself, even if it loses some supposed advantages.

But the crucial outcome would be a free Church, just as all Anglican Churches in the world are free Churches. Perhaps Anglicans forget that the English 'Free Churches' gained the very title of 'Free' in contrast to the perceived captivity (the un-free-ness) of the Church of England. Our rules, our appointments, our conduct ought to be our own responsibility before God, as in 'Free' Church, so that our leaders may lead in these very areas without looking over their shoulders the whole time to see what Parliament might think. To be able to be truly prophetic is to stand absolutely apart from the Government and owe it no favours– that is how church people have discerned their role elsewhere, and we have every reason to want it to be true of us too.

There would be a genuine deliverance in disestablishment. There would be the subtle change of role towards the State. There would be a taking responsibility for ourselves before God. There would be (I trust) a genuine transparency and wide participation in the choosing of bishops. But I suspect the greatest benefit is one rarely discussed – a deliverance from fantasy. The Church of England loves to live by fantasy, it loves to imagine the whole nation of England as Christian and Anglican, to imagine that Parliament is hanging on its words, to imagine that the future must (by divine decree?) be like the past, that any change in the status quo would be disaster, and that disestablishment would make the Church a 'sect'. I long to see an engagement with reality, a view of the nation and the Church of England as God sees them, with the Church engaging in a prophetic confrontation with the ills of society. Here indeed are areas where 'the arm of flesh will fail you', where reliance upon being 'on the inside' of a secularised nation deceives, and where the lingering illusion of power conceals the truth. Establishment has all the qualities of Laodicea – most notably self-deceit. The alternative is much to be desired.

**Notes**

[1] This chapter originates from the Keene Lecture on 'Church and State' that I gave in Chelmsford Cathedral in November 2000.

[2] It is this overview of the period as having the five phases that is the starting-point in the enquiry, and the key to understanding the present day, in my book, *Cut the Connection: the Church of England and Disestablishment*, DLT, 1994, and you will not be surprised that I use it as the key here.

[3] They could only meet when they were convened by the monarch, and could only do business given them by the monarch. The monarch ceased to want them to do business in 1717 (a result of the 'Hoadley affair'), and the Convocations met merely formally, without provision to do business, for 140 years after that.

[4] To this day, the uniting of those sees is visible in bishops of the Church of Ireland who have three or four different names in the title of their bishoprics, and have three or four different cathedrals.

[5] This ended the 'United Church' title and they reverted to being (as they had been before the union of the Parliaments in 1801) two separate institutions—but now as the Church of England, still established, and the Church of Ireland, disestablished and a 'voluntary body'.

[6] Previously they came so regularly as to be almost rhythmical—namely, in the twentieth century, in 1916, 1935, 1952 and 1970.

[7] In my book I publish the fearsome Erastian oath that he has to take, which until quite recently the bishop was not shown until he got there.

[8] Note how it is now taken for grated that there are two entities, and the State has the power of appointment and the Church is the suitor desiring to have some say in the matter.

[9] The composition and processes of the Commission are all under review as I write, but the basic principles remain the same.

[10] As a matter of fact, I suspect that Faculty Jurisdiction (arcane as it is) is actually a bonus that needs extending to all places of worship—and that would, paradoxically, be 'disestablishing', for it would put an end to laws that apply only to the Church of England.

## PART 3

# THE LEADERSHIP REQUIRED

*The stole is the symbol for the towel that our Lord used to dry the disciples'*
*feet after he had washed them on Maundy Thursday. It is worn by the priest*
*to remind him or her of our Lord as the Servant King.*

---

## THE STOLE

My love is to swaddle the babies and pat the old dry,
but you see me hang limply embroidered,
viewed from the pew, narrow and gay.

I loved better the feast with twelve grubby feet,
picked up so gently, by the servant our King,
held gently and kissed and used to wipe dry.

I am the cloth they sling on the floor.
I am used and abused and will take far more–
for I have been held by the King I adore.

*Anna Newton*

---

# 14. Churchwardens

## DAVID FAULL

In what ways can we create the appropriate climate for a healthy balance between vision and realism in church affairs?

How far are individual administrative roles within our churches seen as having the support of a corporate responsibility?

*David Faull, who is now retired, is one of the most experienced and respected Anglican ecclesiastical lawyers alive today. Here he reflects on the crucial role of churchwardens in the Church of England of tomorrow.*

The new Churchwardens Measure emphasises both continuity and a change of emphasis. The Measure itself is dull and unimaginative and one wonders why General Synod wasted time and no doubt considerable amounts of money in introducing it. I am not a cynic, nor am I unduly critical of the General Synod. When I see this sort of Measure, however, I do have some sympathy with St Gregory when he said, in the fourth century, 'For my part, if I am to write the truth, my inclination is to avoid all synods because I have never seen any synod come to a good end nor turn out to be a solution of evils. On the contrary, it usually increases them. You always find there love of contention and love of power which beggars description.' Of course, this cannot be true of deanery synods for they have such little power!

> In this chapter, I propose to refer briefly to the history of churchwardens so that we may know where we have come from before trying to see where we are going. Then I want to look at the Churchwardens Measure 2001, and the debate that it involved. I hope in this way to give some inkling of the different perceptions of Church and State, as well as pointing out some small differences from the existing situation. I then want to take a brief look at the Care of Churches Measure, which demonstrates the substantially new responsibilities that are being placed on churchwardens. Finally, I want to look at the spiritual aspects of the job of a churchwarden, both now and in the future.

## THE HISTORY OF CHURCHWARDENS

A churchwarden's job today is a pale shadow of what it used to be, but, as we shall see, I believe it is once again going to become important. Churchwardens are, in fact, the inheritors of one of the oldest offices in the administrative history of this country. Back in medieval times, they were the primary secular administrators of parishes, and had responsibility for most of the things that local authorities now deal with. Not only were they responsible for the local church, but also for matters of health, education, and so forth. They were often the trustees of major charities. Quite often things still come to light, old trusts are found unadministered or property has been lost, through an accident of history. It is for this reason that the electorate of churchwardens is different from any other electorate in the Church of England, comprising all those whose names are on the church electoral roll of the parish and all who are resident in the parish and whose names are consequently on a register of local government electors.

Churchwardens are thus responsible to a wider group than churchgoers. Like the parish priest, they have a responsibility to the community as a whole. And it is a responsibility that is spiritual as well as administrative. They hold an important position in the community, and, together with the parish priest, they should inform local debate with Christian insights.

## THE CHURCHWARDENS MEASURE 2001

This is the successor to the Churchwardens Measure of 1964 so it is apparent that changes are not often made. To everyone's surprise, the Measure turned out to be highly contentious. Its progress through Parliament throws much light on the relationship between Church and State and the relevant priorities of both. Parliament occasionally shows its teeth as far as church legislation is concerned and the State's old suspicion of the Church, stemming from the days of the Civil War, occasionally raises its head, particularly if the laity are affected. There is still evident mistrust of bishops– quite unfairly, I have to say, in my experience– and when considering this Measure, Parliament saw it as its duty to protect the laity. Many feel that it is not for the State to interfere in Church matters. On the other hand, where legislation is needed, Parliament is bound to have a voice.

The original draft Measure, which closely followed the recommendations made by a working party appointed by the General Synod, was approved by the General Synod. Now the General Synod is a legislative body– as far as I know this country is the only country in the world to have two legislative bodies, both passing legislation– but, and on this occasion it was a big but, all church legislation has to be approved by the Ecclesiastical Committee of Parliament before it can receive the Royal Assent. The Ecclesiastical Committee produces a report on a Measure and if it is favourable, then its report is laid before both Houses of Parliament for approval, and this approval is normally given automatically. If the report of the Ecclesiastical Committee is unfavourable, then the Legislative Committee of the General Synod has the option of withdrawing the Measure.

In the case of the Churchwardens Measure, the Ecclesiastical Committee considered the Measure and expressed serious concern over a clause giving the bishop power to suspend a churchwarden from office. Up until then there had been no such power. The clause stated:

> The Bishop may for any cause which appears to him good and reasonable suspend a person who holds the office of churchwarden... after giving that person sufficient opportunity of showing reason to the contrary.

So concerned was the Ecclesiastical Committee that it requested a joint conference with the General Synod Legislative Committee. It was the phrase 'for any cause which appears to him good and reasonable' that caused problems. In the light of the conference, the Legislative Committee withdrew the Measure and returned it to the General Synod. The General Synod agreed to delete the offending clause and drafted a new one. The revised clause sets out four circumstances in which a person might be suspended, namely:

- if the person concerned requests or consents to suspension, as where there might be a false accusation, the person might ask the bishop to suspend him temporarily;
- where a person is unable to carry out his duties due to illness, incapacity or absence;

- where the person is charged with an offence that is punishable by imprisonment or, if not so, would, if convicted, disqualify that person from being chosen as churchwarden;
- where the churchwarden has been convicted of an offence that is punishable by imprisonment.

All this might appear to be very reasonable and the new clause was taken back to the Ecclesiastical Committee in anticipation that it would be acceptable. Note that the revised clause continued to allow the bishop to suspend in these cases, though there was apparently a right of appeal to the Dean of the Court of Arches.

Because of the seriousness of these matters, and in order to satisfy the Ecclesiastical Committee, a code of practice was drawn up by the House of Bishops setting out principles of guidance to which the bishop must have regard. The Ecclesiastical Committee, however, was not to be so easily satisfied and was not prepared to accept that a code of conduct prepared by the bishops was an acceptable answer to a clause to which they fundamentally objected.

It looked as if a clash between Church and State was inevitable, but in the end, the General Synod decided not to press the matter further for the time being and the Measure went through without the offending clauses. But the General Synod was assured that early in the life of the new Synod, to be elected in the autumn of 2000, steps would be taken to initiate separate legislation covering the power of suspension. So far nothing has happened, but wait for the next thrilling instalment.

I have some sympathy with Parliament. Where suspension or removal from office is concerned, there should be a greater degree of procedure and consultation and this should be set out in the Measure rather than in a code of practice. On the other hand, in this day and age, when public figures have to be above reproach, the reasons for suspension were not unreasonable. But so concerned was Parliament with the rights of churchwardens that it was not considered sufficient to enshrine procedures in a code of practice. That is the way of British justice. You observe Parliament's zeal for freedom of expression. Parliament has on other occasions seen fit to control what it sees as the overweening power of bishops, and churchwardens are undoubtedly seen as the protectors of the people in the pews.

I am sure that bishops feel that they do not have enough power to keep a decent discipline, and in many cases that is true. If bishops' powers are to remain limited, it will increasingly fall to churchwardens to maintain discipline. Churchwardens are the bishop's officers in the parish and it is to the bishop that they must give loyalty. Parliament, however, did not want churchwardens to be fettered.

I have spent some time on this because these matters will become an issue for the future. But it has ever been thus. A story is told that St Augustine was rather worried about a friend of his who had died having led a rather racy life. But St Augustine had a dream in which his friend told him not to worry because all was well– he had crossed the Jordan walking on the heads of bishops.

I now want to look at clause 1 (3) and clause 2 (4) of the Churchwardens Measure, dealing with the question of who is eligible to be a churchwarden. It is stated that the names of potential churchwardens must be on the electoral roll of the parish– it is no longer enough to be resident; they must be communicant members of the church, unless the bishop agrees otherwise; they must be twenty-one or over; they must have signified their consent to serve; and they must have no disqualifications prescribed by the Measure.

It is the clause that allows the bishop to give permission for non-communicant church members to be churchwardens that may affect churchwardens in the future. This might occur where there is a shared church, or, say, where a nonconformist attends a church, is a useful member of the parish, but does not wish to be confirmed. This raises questions of theology and will, I am sure, give some pause for thought. It raises questions about how far bishops are of the esse of the Church. It goes much further than merely allowing communicant members of other Churches to take communion. On balance, I believe that it is the right way forward in the twenty-first century, but the question always has to be asked: 'Why should a person who is sufficiently committed to become a churchwarden, that is, to hold the principal lay office in the church, not want to be confirmed?' These are issues that must be grappled with.

But section 2 (4) goes further when it says, 'All rules of law whereby certain persons are disqualified from being chosen for the office of churchwarden shall cease to have effect.' I wonder if this clause has been wholly understood. It used to be the law that foreigners and Jews could not be churchwardens but it is now legally possible for a Jew, a Roman Catholic or, presumably, a Muslim to become a churchwarden if consent is given by the bishop. Whether the Jew, Roman Catholic or Muslim would be allowed to remain a member of his or her own faith is another question. As the years go by these issues will have to be faced, and I wonder what it says to our own faith in Jesus Christ that we can so lightly pass legislation that at least gives rise to the possibility of someone of another faith being able to be a churchwarden. There is everything to be said for welcoming foreigners, outsiders and peoples of all or no faiths– it is, indeed, part of our Christian tradition– but surely to be able to hold office, people should be committed believers, even if they are of a tradition other than our own.

Finally, it may come as a relief to many churchwardens to know that a person can now resign as churchwarden (previously churchwardens could not resign). Also, as a general rule, under the new legislation churchwardens only serve for six years– so it is not the life sentence that it has so often been in the past.

## THE CARE OF CHURCHES AND
## ECCLESIASTICAL JURISDICTION MEASURE, 1991

Now it would be wrong to ignore the question of buildings when considering the role of churchwardens. This is an enormous subject in itself, so in this chapter I will only consider it from one angle.

The question of church buildings will increasingly occupy churchwardens as we move further into the twenty-first century. Most of our buildings are listed and are of enormous value to the spiritual environment of a community. Care of the buildings is a very great responsibility that sooner rather than later the Church must address. As congregations get smaller, how are they to raise the money to repair these vitally important buildings? It is amazing what is achieved. My little village in Cornwall, with a winter population of about three hundred people, has recently raised well in excess of £500,000 simply to restore its medieval roof.

Up until a few years ago, churches were often neglected or merely kept safe, but the Care of Churches Measure has placed a duty on churchwardens and the PCC to apply for a faculty to restore and repair churches. An entirely new procedure is set out in which, although churchwardens are not specifically mentioned, they clearly have very substantial responsibilities. Section 13 (1) of the Measure says:

> If in any proceedings by any person for obtaining a faculty, it appears to the Consistory Court that any other person being a party to the proceedings, or joined into the proceedings, was responsible wholly or in part for any act or default in consequence of which the proceedings were instituted, the court may order the whole or any part of the costs and expenses of the proceedings or consequent thereon, including the expenses of any work authorised by the faculty (so far as any such cost or expenses have been occasioned by that act or default), to be paid by the persons responsible.

The Measure stipulates that failure to comply with any order will be treated as contempt of Court.

This Measure is aimed at many people: the archdeacon, the PCC , the church-wardens, and individual parishioners. In effect, it says that if anything is very wrong with a church building, or work is being done without a faculty, or ornaments are being disposed of without a faculty, and someone is aware of this and does not attempt to put it right, then that person could be personally liable. This is not entirely new, but in the past the law has had no teeth to compel the offending person or persons to do the work. The Department of the Environment is determined that important buildings shall be repaired and made it very clear that unless the Church passed some very tough legislation the faculty jurisdiction would be removed and churches would be at the mercy of the local authority.

There are many who think that the upkeep and repair of churches should be the responsibility of local residents through the council tax, but that is not the view of the Church authorities, except in the case of buildings that the Church might wish to make redundant. Real responsibility, therefore, rests on the shoulders of churchwardens, far more so than in the past. These valuable buildings are there and must be cared for.

The main job of each local church is to preach the gospel, to enable people to worship, and to carry out work that Christ adjures us to do, but these are the buildings in which the Lord is worshipped and they must be kept worthy of him. The Church is going to have to raise more and more money to pay the clergy, and more and more money to repair and restore buildings, so these matters will occupy more and more time. Priorities, both practical and theological, will have to be assessed and sometimes decisions will be painful. We cannot lightly pull down buildings where prayer and worship have been said for centuries, but we have to pay and house the clergy, and we have to give to the poor and destitute. Some buildings, therefore, will have to go, and churchwardens will have the responsibility of guiding the parish through negotiations involving redundancies. It is a challenge that I believe is coming from the Lord. I am sure the challenge can be met, but much of this century will be spent doing just that.

I would stress that there need be no alarm over the powers in the Care of

Churches Measure. As local churches work with architects and their dioceses, all these things can be handled. It is only where people are deliberately negligent or ignore the advice they are given that trouble will arise.

## THE SPIRITUAL WORK OF CHURCHWARDENS

But churchwardens have other important responsibilities. One of the canons of the Church of England, Canon E1 (3), states:

> Churchwardens shall be foremost in representing the laity and in cooperating with the incumbent; they shall use their best endeavours, by example and precept, to encourage parishioners in the practice of true religion and to promote unity and peace among them.

So there is a very important spiritual side to the work of a churchwarden and this, it seems to me, will become increasingly important. As I have said, churchwardens are primarily the bishops' officers and ultimately it is to bishops that they owe their primary duty. But in my experience there are more tensions in parishes today than ever before. This is due partly to the pace of life, partly to increasing materialism and sometimes to the isolation of the clergy. Occasionally clergy find it necessary to make changes in forms of worship or to challenge people very seriously, and this is not always appreciated by those who remember the more comfortable days of the Church of England when there was a good bit of respectable hymn singing, a short sermon and everybody could be away home in time to enjoy a glass of sherry by midday.

On the whole, people take their faith more seriously these days. Moreover, in these changing times, respect for authority is diminishing, and sadly the incumbent is all too often at odds with church members. When this happens, churchwardens are there to hold people and priest together. They must support the priest in so far as they can and try to represent his position to the people and the people's position to him or her. The churchwarden's job is to try to heal rifts. Supporting the parish priest, however, does not mean agreeing over everything. When faced with problems, churchwardens and priest should pray and study the Bible together. All this may seem obvious, but I have found that, instead of remaining neutral, churchwardens often side with one party or the other. Their role in disputes is vital and time-consuming, but disagreements often end in reconciliation, which is really what the gospel is all about. As a last resort, churchwardens can go to the archdeacon or the bishop, but when it reaches that level, the disagreement is often too bitter for reconciliation.

## MINISTRY AND ADMINISTRATION

One archdeacon has referred to the role of churchwarden as 'management, maintenance and ministry'. Another has described it as 'leadership, labour and love'. I prefer the former because of the reference to ministry. I believe that the work of ministering to the church is going to become an increasingly important part of the churchwarden's job.

I also believe that a church that is administratively right is pastorally right. There is nothing more irritating to those on the fringe of the church than bad administration. It does not honour God and, indeed, it drives people away from his church.

In this chapter, I have wandered through many byways of the Church's life, but I have been trying to say that while many changes are taking place, churchwardens remain a constant. Their job is simply to be there, through all the vicissitudes, to represent the ongoing life of the church, and to encourage and look after the people, however difficult the times may be. Their opportunities to serve the Lord have never been greater.

# 15. Enabling local leaders

## AMIEL OSMASTON

Is it possible in Church of England parishes to develop effective forms of shared leadership? Can clergy and laity be weaned away from their fears, habits and the defence of their privileges, to enable this to happen?

Many churches have tried to create a Body of Christ pattern of 'shared ministry'. Sadly, this often degenerates into clergy delegating jobs to the laity. True shared ministry can only flourish where it is stimulated and reasourced by shared leadership.

*Amiel Osmaston serves in the Diocese of Carlisle as Ministry Development Officer, working with clergy and laity. In this paper she draws on her recent experience of seven years as Ministry Development Officer in the Diocese of Chester, as well as her previous posts in parish ministry as the Director of Mission and Pastoral Studies at Ridley Hall, Cambridge.*

*Here she shares her vision for local ministry teams trained to seek God's way forward and to encourage all church members into the ministry, service and outreach[1].*

### THE STARTING POINT?

My own starting point is that good leadership is essential for the life and health of the Church. In order to express the corporate nature of the Body of Christ, this leadership should be shared, with clergy and lay people working together. I am passionately committed to enabling local leaders and to developing leadership teams. My own experience has reinforced these convictions, and given me the opportunity to put them into practice.

My experiences, however, have also shown me the dangers of coming from the wrong starting point. Although it is exciting that many dioceses and parishes are seeking to build up local leadership, it can be very destructive if this is done for the wrong reasons. Unfortunately many are driven by need and fear (falling finances; expensively-crumbling buildings; fewer clergy, each increasingly overstretched and frantically propping up the system; declining and ageing congregations in many places, etc.). Faced with all this, we tend to look at what needs to be done in order to maintain the system, then identify the jobs that the clergy haven't time to do, and delegate them to the laity. Jobs are often dumped on to lay people with no training or support. This is not surprising, as most clergy have not been taught how to enable their lay leaders.

Traditionally, the Church of England has seen parish leadership as being largely the preserve of the clergy. This means that when we do try to develop local lay leaders, we often give the impression that they are an unfortunate necessity, second-rate props brought in to shore up a tottering clericalised institution. It is therefore not surprising if many potential local leaders are reluctant and lack enthusiasm, confidence or vision.

The starting point must rather be that the enabling of local leadership by clergy and laity is good in itself. It must not spring out of negativity and fear, but out of the conviction that Christian leadership must be shared if it is to have integrity and to reflect the nature of the God we claim to serve. But more of that later...

## A QUICK PREVIEW

To help you decide whether to read the rest of this chapter, here is a quick outline of my intentions. I shall start with principles and then follow them through to practicalities. The journey will cover:

- *A parable* to highlight the needs.
- *The purpose of it all* – if we are going to grow local leaders, what will they be expected to lead the Church into being and doing? What are the vision and the priorities?
- *The people we need* – who will these local leaders be? How can we discern their gifts and calling, and motivate them to offer themselves.
- *Training* – how can we grow potential leaders into mature and Christlike qualities of character, as well as equipping them with knowledge

and practical skills?

- *Tasking, trusting and tending* – how can the local leaders be properly resourced and supported, rather than merely abandoned to get on with it all?
- *Can this enabling of local leaders actually be done in practice?* Yes! I shall end by describing a strategy for the development of local ministry and leadership in the Diocese of Chester, drawing some lessons from this.

## A PARABLE OF ELEPHANTS

Many years ago, when I was indulging in being a hippie, I wandered into the depths of a large forest in Northern Thailand. I happened to stumble across an elephant training centre, and was so fascinated that I decided to stay for a few days. The elephants were being trained in all the complex skills required for working in the logging industry. I watched as a new young elephant was 'broken in'. First she was shackled by a long chain to a gigantic forest tree. For three days she rampaged around, straining at her chain and flattening everything in a wide circle around the tree. Eventually she settled down and seemed to become accustomed to her chain. A mahout told me that after a few months she would become so familiar with the length of her chain that she would automatically stay within its range. From then on, the elephant would not need to be chained to a tree or even a stout stake. The chain could merely be attached to a flimsy peg in the ground, and the elephant would still not go beyond her chain length. She would be chained largely by habit and by ingrained expectations.

Can leaders become chained in a similar way? Many church leaders (clergy and lay) seem to have become bound by habit, convention and ingrained self-limitations. We have given up exploring and testing the limits. We have grown comfortable with a limited sphere of movement and a short range of vision. We stick to the familiar stamping grounds of what is known and safe.

What is worse, we (the existing leadership) create new leaders in our own image. Potential leaders are selected partly on the basis that they will be manageable and will adapt themselves contentedly to the limitations of the system. Their training then equips them to operate within the range of the chain, but not beyond.

When Stephen defended himself against the Sanhedrin, the religious leaders of his day (Acts 7), he reminded them of the God of the Exodus, the God who leads his people out of bondage into the unknown. And yet the people 'in their hearts turned back to Egypt' (verse 39) to the secure familiarities of bondage. Stephen concludes:

> However, the Most High does not live in houses made by men.
> As the prophet says:
> 'Heaven is my throne, and the earth is my footstool.
> What kind of house will you build for me? Says the Lord.
> Or where will my resting place be?' . . .
> You stiff-necked people!
>
> *Acts 7: 48-51 NIV*

Stirring stuff! And they stoned him for it. What is our response to the same challenge now? Unlike the elephant, do we dare to uproot the stake and wake up to the possibilities of where God might wish to lead us?

And yet.. leaders must be realistic too. It is naïve to think that the Church of England can undo hundreds of years of history and revert to being a movement rather than a fixed institution. All movements become institutions if they survive long enough. Yet if we are to be faithful to our God, we must deliberately keep working to counteract the fossilising pressures that are part of institutionalisation. Are our leaders open to hear God's call to pull up the stake and move on when that is necessary? If they are not, we will fail to respond to our changing cultural needs and challenges, and the Church will become an irrelevant white elephant on the bric-a-brac stall.

How can we enable and equip local leaders (clergy and laity) who will dare to lead the Church forward into God's future, and not simply cling to preserving the familiar stamping grounds of the status quo? The rest of this chapter is an attempt to answer that question.

## DISCERNING GOD'S PURPOSE
## AND PEOPLE THROUGH PRAYER

This section is not abstract theorising. It is based on a project for training local leadership teams in parishes in the Diocese of Chester. This 'Partners in Leadership' programme has been developed over four years and well tested in practice. I will describe its method and application at the end of the chapter, but in this section I will set out the principles that undergird it.

The 'Partners in Leadership' programme was initiated by James Newcome (previously Director of Ministry in the Chester Diocese, now Bishop of Penrith, and also a contributor to this volume), and me, together with a large team of excellent advisers, consultants and trainers. We did a considerable amount of research into leadership training, including visiting and learning from most of the Anglican dioceses that already have programmes for training local leadership/ministry teams.

We found a great deal of good practice. Much effective leadership is being exercised through the traditional structures of clergy, wardens, standing committees, PCCs, etc., as well as through the newer ministry teams, leadership teams, pastoral oversight groups, etc. Nearly all these groups, however, seemed to be weighed down by the demands of maintenance ministry– simply keeping the Church's activities going. Very few had the time or the training to ask the key leadership questions about overall purpose, priorities and vision. Very few had the time or the training to help discern and equip other potential lay leaders and ministers within the congregation. Very few PCCs or leadership groups gave a significant amount of time to prayer. As a result of this research, we designed the training of our 'Partners in Leadership' teams to focus primarily on these three neglected areas of purpose, people and prayer.

## Prayer

A Christian who is called to leadership, whether in a church or secular context, must be a person who is committed to prayer. A leader must spend time listening to God, to discern God's will and way forward in each situation, and to see how and where God is already at work. The leader's tasks of discerning God's purposes and identifying potential people who could help to implement these purposes, cannot be fulfilled without much prayer. Individual and corporate commitment to prayer has always been the seedbed of revival and growth in God's Church. Therefore a vital part of enabling local leaders, is to teach them to pray, and to make time for regular and extensive prayer together.

## Purpose

A leader must be leading people towards/into/for something. There must be a direction, a purpose, a sense of movement and progress. To achieve this, there needs to be a sense of shared vision. We must beware of the elephant trap of self-imposed limitations on our movements and vision. Our concern for our local community often leads us to focus too narrowly and rapidly on local needs and opportunities. This is likely to limit our vision. We must start by asking wider questions in an attempt to paint the big picture of God's overall purposes, from which must flow the local incarnation of that vision.

- We cannot know what kind of leadership is required (or how it can be enabled) until we know God's purposes for his Church;
- we cannot know the purpose of the Church until we know God's purposes for his Kingdom, which the Church seeks to build;
- we cannot know the nature and purposes of God's Kingdom, until we grasp the character, nature and purposes of the God whose will constitutes that Kingdom.

In other words, if we want to grasp God's purposes for our local context, and to lead his people faithfully into fulfilling those purposes, then we must look first at the character of God himself. Only then will we be able to make deductions about the nature of God's Kingdom and hence the purpose and calling of God's Church, universally and locally. The continual task of Christian leaders must be to keep asking: If the nature of God/the Kingdom/the Church is X (for example, giving freedom to the oppressed), then what are God's purposes and priorities in this place, at this moment? What is his calling to us, here and now?

It is usually dangerous for a leader or group of leaders to see themselves as the sole authorities on God's purposes for the local context. It is vital that vision-forming should be done corporately and collaboratively. People will not be committed to implementing a vision if they have not shared in forming it. It is vital that the whole local church should grasp the big picture of the purposes of God, the Kingdom and the universal Church. This gives a sense of perspective to local activities and builds motivation as people feel that they are part of God's wider eternal purposes. Leaders must be trained in the complex processes of leading a church through the journey of consultation, discussion and vision-forming.

Leaders must also be trained in the continuous process of checking and appraising all the local church's activities in the light of the vision, purposes and priorities that have been agreed. The church may be doing some things merely out of tradition and habit, and these need to stop if they do not contribute to God's present purposes for this church. This will then liberate people and time for more strategic and effective ministry.

### People

It is a waste of time to discern God's purposes for the local context, if there are then no people to implement them. Many church leaders operate on the basis of having a good idea ( 'We ought to start a toddler group, in order to attract young families'), and then asking for volunteers or twisting people's arms to carry it out. This can be fatal, landing the wrong people in the wrong roles and causing endless problems for the future.

A key role of leaders is to discern who has been called by God to which responsibilities and ministries. The theological basis for this is that all the baptised are called to ministry in the Church and the world. Many of them are called to exercise some leadership within that area of ministry. So Christian leaders must be enablers of the leadership and ministry of others. A repeated emphasis in the New Testament is that God gives gifts to all his people (1 Corinthians 12). These gifts must be developed and used for building God's Church and establishing God's Kingdom (Ephesians 4:11-16).

The discernment of gifts cannot be done in isolation. It must be a corporate process. Leaders must take the time to get to know people and gain their trust. It is tragic that so many Christians who are extremely capable in their everyday lives, seem to lack any confidence that they might have something of spiritual significance to offer. How can we motivate people to offer themselves for ministry and leadership? They need to be enabled to discover their gifts and to grow in their knowledge of God's love and calling to them. (A practical point: there are some resources which can help congregations to achieve this. I commend the Willow Creek network material[2]. Also, I am currently developing a short course for parish groups, to enable them to help each other discern their gifts, abilities, personality, experiences and longings, which may indicate the kinds of ministry to which God is calling them.) There is a great need for this sort of discerning and confidence-building exercise. British people are normally very bad at affirming one another, and are often unaware of their own strengths. There are tremendous resources for ministry and leadership that are waiting to be discovered and liberated.

The issue of identifying peoples' gifts is closely linked to the issues of identifying God's purposes for the Church (discussed above). Once a whole church has begun to catch a glimpse of what God is calling it to be and do, then individuals can find their place within those purposes. A strong sense of motivation comes from seeing one's own small contribution as part of something bigger that God is doing. God has promised to equip his Church with the necessary gifts, so once a church has some idea of what he is wanting for its local context, then it can pray for God to give the gifts and direct the church to the people who will be able to fulfil these purposes.

The whole process of discernment through prayer of God's purposes and people is absolutely vital. The process, however, does not end there. Once the right people have been discerned for particular areas of ministry and leadership, they need to be enabled, trained, liberated, equipped and supported. The next section looks at some ways in which this can be done.

**Training**

It is vital that local leaders are trained and equipped for the tasks to which they are called. A very high percentage of the financial resources of the Church of England go into providing for the initial training of clergy. Comparatively little is spent on continuing ministerial education (CME) to provide opportunities for life-long learning in ministry and leadership. Even less money is spent on the initial or continuing training of lay leaders within the Church. The priority given to this varies enormously from one diocese to another. Thus, for example, some dioceses have only a handful of readers, whereas others have five hundred or more. Some dioceses train and enable a wide range of authorised or informal lay ministries, whereas other dioceses have virtually none.

The training that is offered by dioceses and parishes to their Christian leaders varies enormously in scope and quality. There is a great deal of excellent training on offer. However, there is an unfortunate tendency towards narrow pragmatism. A necessary job is identified, and then people are simply taught the skills for that job. They are often not given the background knowledge and resources to enable them to operate flexibly, respond to new circumstances, and keep growing and developing. This emphasis on skills can lead to rigid patterns of leadership and maintenance-ministry, as people fear to move beyond the security of their own skills base. (Remember the elephant!)

It is vital that the training and enabling of local leaders should be holistic. Leaders must be trained not only in 'doing', but in 'knowing' and 'being'. Hands, head and heart must all be involved.

**1. Training in 'being' (the heart)**

Leaders must be enabled to grow into maturity and Christ-likeness in their character, qualities, attitudes, holiness, etc. To achieve this, training must be formational and transformational. The method of training must build relationships and foster openness and honesty. This is easier to achieve if the learning takes place with a regular group over a long period of time, or is at least partly residential. Leaders must be helped to grow in 'emotional intelligence' (see Daniel Goleman[3]) and the ability to relate to others in a mature and creative way. Leadership is essentially relational. Within his own nature, as the three-in-one of the holy Trinity, our God exercises authority and leadership in relationship. Our leadership must mirror this.

When I was teaching ordinands, the staff of each theological college were asked to write a detailed response to the Church of England's paper 'ACCM 22' on the aims of training. The specific question we faced was 'What ordained ministry does the Church of England require?' We identified certain qualities and attitudes that our training should seek to develop in potential ministers and leaders. I shall quote from this list as it is equally relevant to the training of ordained and lay leaders.

The lifelong journey towards 'the full stature of Christ' (Ephesians 4:13) includes many different dimensions. No list can be exhaustive, but we particularly seek the development of the following Christlike qualities and attitudes:

- A growing appetite for God, fed by a disciplined life of prayer, and burgeoning into a visible and infectious love for God
- An expectant faith which believes that God is at work in the world
- A confidence in the Christian gospel and its capacity to change peoples' lives
- An emotional and spiritual security rooted in Christ, enabling one to reach out in sacrificial love to others
- An intellectual integrity, engaging honestly with profound issues, and being prepared to lives with unsolved questions
- A commitment to consider carefully and respectfully the views of those with whom one disagrees, and discernment about when to engage in controversy

- A compassion for those in need, and a passion for justice
- Love, evidenced by graciousness in speech and action, accessibility and empathy
- An ability to challenge, correct and rebuke where necessary
- A readiness both to exercise and submit to authority in a constructive way
- A commitment to plan and work with other people both within church life and beyond
- A loving realism about the Church, including an appreciation of the riches of the Anglican tradition
- An ability to spark off change and to handle the dynamics of change
- Self-knowledge about one's personality, history and sexuality, and how one interacts with others
- Awareness of one's strengths and weaknesses, with a capacity to learn from failure as well as success, issuing in an appropriate confidence and humility
- The capacity to cope with disappointment without losing hope
- A commitment to grow in personal holiness, marked by the blossoming of the 'fruit of the Spirit' (Galatians 5:22-23), and being equipped for the realities of spiritual warfare
- The practice of a balanced lifestyle with regard to family, friends, money, home, possessions, work and leisure.
- The formation of these qualities and attitudes are both a gift of God and a discipline to be worked out in individual and corporate life.

When we speak of enabling local leaders, we must ensure that the training we provide for them is carefully designed to help them grow in these qualities and attitudes.

### 2. Training in 'knowing' (the head)
It is crucial that leaders be equipped with a firm foundation of knowledge about their faith. They also need a good knowledge of all the areas that are relevant to the particular ministry and leadership they are called to exercise, and a thorough knowledge of the local context with its history, characteristics, people and needs. In addition to all this, they must know where/to

whom to go to find further knowledge and resources.

Another important area of training in knowledge, is equipping people with the knowledge of how to make everyday connections between faith and action, belief and behaviour. It is particularly important that Christian leaders have integrity and that what they say is mirrored by what they do. Leaders are particularly vulnerable to charges of hypocrisy, and this undermines the witness of the gospel. Often this is unintentional, and simply stems from not having the time or the knowledge to look at the implications of faith for action, and conversely the implications of experiences for beliefs. Training in the processes of reflective learning or 'practical theology' can make a huge contribution to the integrity of the Church's leadership.

### 3. Training in 'doing' (the hands)

In spite of my disparaging comments earlier about the dangers of training that is merely skills-based, it is vital that the training and enabling of local leaders should include equipping them with the skills and abilities and abilities they need. It is alarming how often people are 'volunteered' into taking on a particular role or responsibility on the assumption that they will be able to get on and do it. There is an unfortunate culture of amateurishness in the Church. We 'make do' and muddle along. The bumbling PCC in 'The Vicar of Dibley' sometimes comes uncomfortably close to reality!

It is true that as the Body of Christ we must welcome the contribution of each member of the Body, even the weakest. If that contribution, however, is to be a worthy offering to God, it needs to be nurtured, grown, pruned and shaped by careful training and encouragement. Talents must be improved and extended so that God is glorified by the best that we can offer.

I believe that most Christian leaders (clergy and lay) would benefit enormously from having a mentor. It can be extremely helpful to meet regularly with a wise and more experienced Christian leader for reflection and discussion. Normally the mentor should be somebody engaged in a similar kind of ministry/leadership, but, in order to provide objectivity, outside one's own local context. Another useful model is that of apprenticeship, where one learns alongside another leader by observing, helping and improving through practice and feedback.

As with training leaders in 'being' and 'knowing', the training in 'doing' must be a never-ending process. However good and experienced we become at doing something, we can always improve further. Humility and a lifelong desire to learn are perhaps the most important of the qualities needed by growing Christian disciples who are called to leadership.

## TASKING, TRUSTING AND TENDING

When people agree to take on particular responsibilities and tasks, it is not enough simply to train them. There must be an ongoing structure of support and accountability. The next three sections will look at some essential elements of that structure under the headings of tasking, trusting and tending. These are based on Gillian Stamp's concept of the 'tripod of work'. Like the legs of a three-legged stool, tasking, trusting and tending must each must be strongly established, or the work stool will collapse.

### Tasking

When someone is given a leadership responsibility, it is vital to clarify the task that needs to be done, and to show why and how it is to be done. If this does not happen, then a mismatch of expectations is likely to cause frustration or hurt later. Many Christian leaders have such a vague and open-ended 'job description', that their zeal drives them to exhaustion while still making them feel guilty for not doing more. No wonder so many Christian leaders are stressed, neglect their families and become disillusioned. If we claim to be preaching a gospel of grace, we should live it!

There is a useful mnemonic from industry that is worth borrowing here. Our tasking needs to be SMART:

**Specific:**    be clear about what we want to achieve

**Measured:**    put numbers to it if possible, for example, by how much do we want to grow? What criteria will we use to measure growth?

**Achievable:** is the proposed task sensible and achievable in general?

**Realistic:** have we got the necessary resources of people, time, money, etc., here and now?

**Timed:** set targets and an end point to the task or to the person's period of responsibility.

Of course, plans are always provisional and tasks may need to be changed in the light of experience, and developments. A clear definition of the task, however, does not need to cause inflexibility, as it can form the basis for renewed discussion whenever the person's role is reviewed.

### Trusting

If the leadership is to be creative and fruitful, the leader must be trusted with responsibility, and encouraged to exercise initiative, not just be given a list of set tasks. There must also be accountability. It is important to be clear about the level of responsibility and initiative that is expected. All leaders should be 'under authority' and receive some kind of supervision. Even Jesus saw himself as under the authority of his Father.

> It is important that accountability should be clear and mutual. Leaders are accountable upwards as well as downwards– to their supervisor as well as to those whom they lead and serve. Too many clergy/supervisors are insecure in their own role and so tend to over-control or interfere in the work of local lay leaders. This is just as destructive as the opposite error of abandoning them to their own devices, to sink or swim.

### Tending

Tending is particularly vital when dealing with volunteers. After all, they are not paid to do the job, so they need to be motivated and encouraged in other ways. It is important that the person who is supervising local leaders should:

- ove and get to know those leaders– value them for themselves, not just for what they are doing;
- keep regular contact;

- thank them frequently and acknowledge their role publicly;
- hold people's hands' if they need it, support them and build up their confidence;
- accept and use failure, helping them to see every failure as a learning opportunity. This attitude enables people to continue to take creative risks. Effective tending is vital if a local leader is to be enabled to grow into maturity with the necessary attitudes and qualities of character for leadership (see the list set out earlier).

A useful practical resource for helping the Church with the process of tasking, trusting and tending local leaders and ministers is the report/workbook published by the Society of Mary and Martha, entitled *Affirmation and Accountability*[4].

> It is interesting to look at John 21:15-22 where Jesus, speaking to Peter by the lake after the resurrection, asks, 'Do you love me?... Feed my sheep.' It is a wonderful example of Jesus tasking, trusting and tending simultaneously as he lovingly reinstates Peter and trusts him with a vital task.

## PUTTING THEORY INTO PRACTICE: A STRATEGY FOR ENABLING LOCAL LEADERSHIP IN THE DIOCESE OF CHESTER

It would be wonderful if everything that I have described so far could be done effectively at parish level. Many clergy, however, feel that their own leadership is not being adequately resourced, and that they do not have enough time, energy or ability to resource the leadership of others. Therefore in most parishes the enabling of local leaders would benefit from some external resourcing at deanery or diocesan level.

In my role as Ministry Development Officer in the Diocese of Chester I was privileged to be part of the growth of a culture of training for local leadership and ministry. The initial impetus for this was given by the previous Bishop of Chester, Michael Baughen, and it has grown through the work and vision of many people over the past fifteen years.

The aim has been to equip both laity and clergy more effectively as leaders/ministers, and to enable them to work better together. The training of the two groups proceeded separately at first, in order to build confidence and to provide a foundation of the necessary attitudes, knowledge and skills. As these have become established, clergy and lay leaders have increasingly been trained together.

Mature leaders cannot be grown overnight, and the process has to start at the grassroots. Fifteen years ago, the Bishop initiated a year-long 'Bishop's Course in Christian Faith and Life'. (Fifteen evening sessions in small local groups, plus three big day conferences.) It encouraged people to discuss their faith in more depth and apply it practically to their everyday lives. It also emphasised that all Christians are called to be disciples, life-long learners and ministers. People learnt to put their beliefs into words, they grew in confidence, and their views were challenged and broadened by engaging with people from other parishes. The course expanded people's understanding of ministry, the Church and their God, and made them feel part of an exciting diocesan-wide vision.

Since then, over 3,000 people have done the Bishop's Course. It is striking that over this time there has been a huge increase in lay ministry, and that nearly all of those who have been authorised as readers, parish assistants or parish evangelists in the last few years were launched into the journey towards ministry by doing the Bishop's Course. The course created a hunger for spiritual growth and continued learning, together with a deeper commitment to serve God in the Church and the world. 'Graduates' of the course demanded more, so the diocese started offering a whole *smorgasbord* of short courses each year on a huge variety of topics relevant to faith and ministry. Between them, the courses offered a wide range of training in knowledge, attitudes and skills. The aim was to create a range of resources for lifelong learning.

Learning breeds learning, and the desire continued to grow. A category of authorised lay ministry was created, called parish assistants. These were potential leaders already serving God in pastoral or organisational roles, who were put forward by their parishes for diocesan training and commissioning. A two-year training course was devised.

Many clergy and lay leaders began to feel that greater mutual trust and team-work was needed. Learning together is clearly one of the best ways of developing mutual trust and respect for one another's differing skills and ministries. Therefore it was decided to start training all lay leaders together, and to involve their clergy in this as much as possible. So in 1998, the 'Foundations for Ministry Course' was created as the common first year of training for all readers, parish assistants and parish evangelists (the role of PEs was established at this time). The course focuses on the nature of the Kingdom, the Church and ministry in contemporary society, encouraging the discernment of gifts, teamwork and shared leadership. The course is challenging and demanding, and is validated at Level 1 by Chester College. Many people start the course as independent candidates, and in the process discover a vocation to ministry as a reader, PA or PE. It is enormously encouraging to see how people have grown through this course, releasing a huge amount of ministry in the parishes, and the development of many ministry teams. Eighty people per year have done the course, and it has made a huge contribution to the growth of ministry and mission.

While this whole strategy for developing lay ministry and leadership has ben progressing, there has been a parallel strategy for equipping clergy to exercise more effective leadership, and teaching them to enable their lay leaders. In 1995, a carefully selected group of clergy were invited to attend a 'Getting Fit For Growth' course. This was enthusiastically received, the word spread, demand gradually increased, and it has now developed into 'The Chester Leadership Development Programme', consisting of six three-day modules spread over two years. The course aims to transform any negative attitudes (for example, fear of the loss of role/status/power; fear of risk-taking; loss of vision, etc.) and to build skills in strategy and vision-forming, shared leadership and effective ministry and mission.

These two parallel strategies, working with laity and clergy, began to bear fruit. To promote the growing sense of mutual trust and shared leadership, most in-service training events for clergy were opened to all authorised lay ministers. Also, as a sign of the diocese's valuing of lay ministry, all authorised lay ministers were offered the same annual in-service training grant as clergy.

At first there was some defensiveness from clergy, but most of this has now dissipated as people have discovered that the experience of learning is vastly enriched when ordained and lay leaders are involved in it together.

As clergy and laity have begun to work more closely together in learning, ministry, mission and leadership, parishes began to ask for help with establishing local leadership teams. So in 1999 the Director of Ministry (James Newcome) and I began to work with a number of other advisers and trainers in developing the 'Partners in Leadership Programme'.

The programme involves the diocese in working closely with individual parishes to help them discern, establish and train a leadership team. This is only done at the request of the parish, and after a nine-month consultancy process that ensures that the incumbent, PCC and all church members understand and support the strategy. Each parish has different needs and is likely to develop a different kind of team. However the primary focus of the Partners in Leadership Programme is not to develop management teams to 'run the church'. The team is designed to be a resource to the PCC, advising on issues of vision, ministry and mission. The primary focus of the leadership team would be:

- *Purpose*: Enabling the church to develop its vision, clarify its priorities in the light of that vision, and assess its activities against those priorities.
- *People*: Helping others to discern their gifts; ensuring that those gifts are being used effectively, and supporting their ministries in the world as well as in the church.
- *Prayer*: Listening to God, seeking discernment and praying for the life and mission of the church.

The diocese provides two trainers (one ordained and one lay) who come into the parish and train the leadership team intensively over a period of six months. The vicar receives training with everyone else, as a member of the leadership team.

So far, twelve parishes have completed the full two-year programme and have commissioned their leadership teams. It has been very exciting to see the high level of commitment to the vision for shared leadership and the way in which the teams seem to be acting as catalysts for the growth of ministry and mission in their parishes.

## POSTSCRIPT

There is still a long way to go in improving the ways in which the Church enables local leaders. One obvious difficulty is that this commitment to training is costly in terms of money, time and staff. Like most dioceses, the Chester Diocese is currently under a certain amount of financial pressure. There have been some reductions and changes in diocesan staffing and therefore in the training programmes that can be resourced. A review of the work of ministry, education and training has been instigated by the diocesan bishop. New priorities and opportunities are likely to develop, and the 'pathway of learning' that has been described above will continue to change and evolve.

In closing, I want to encourage you to believe that it is possible to change the culture of a parish/area/diocese so that local leadership is enabled. Over time the cumulative effects of this can snowball into really significant growth in ministry and mission. I have been privileged to see this happening, and I hope I have encouraged you to believe that it could happen in your context too.

**Notes**

[1] This chapter is based on material given at a symposium on 18 September, 2001, at St Deiniol's, Hawarden, North Wales, on 'The Church of England: where is it going?'

[2] Bruce Bugbee, Don Cousins and Bill Hybels, *Network: The right people... in the right place ...for the right reaons*, Willow Creek Resources, Zondervan Publishing House, Grand Rapids, Michigan, 1994.

[3] Daniel Golemann, *Emotional Intelligence*, Bloomsbury Press, 1995.

[4] *Affirmation and Accountability*, published in 2002 by the Society of Mary and Martha, Sheldon, Dunsford, Exeter, EX6 7LE. Tel. 017647 252752.

# 16. The priesthood of all believers— yes, even the laity!

## ROY CALVOCORESSI

Are there ways in which we can quietly stand against the prevailing political system in order to give voice to the priesthood of the laity?

Is the concept of Christianisation at variance with the principle of a singularly Anglican form of church life?

*Roy Calvocoressi is the founder and Director of CHIPS (Christian International Peace Service), and was awarded an OBE in the Golden Jubilee Birthday Honours for this work. Before going to Cyprus to start his work for CHIPS, he served on the PCC of All Souls, Langham Place. He became a founder trustee of Traidcraft.*

*Here Roy challenges a church-centred vision of ministry with an orientation towards Christ's coming Kingdom in the whole world and suggests that recovering the doctrine of the priesthood of all believers is a key in this process.*

### INTRODUCTION

#### a. Four main aspects

Lay priesthood is strangely under-developed in the Church of England. Its least developed aspect is the introduction of Christian ways, ideas, values and principles to the whole process of industry, commerce, and other areas of the secular world. This process is referred to in this chapter as 'Christianisation'.

A more obvious aspect of lay priesthood is sharing in the ministry of the parish work of the church, sometimes including the lay presidency of the Eucharist.

Providing help for those who are most disadvantaged in society is a third aspect of lay priesthood, and one that is much more prevalent but in some cases needs to move on from ministry to priesthood, as in the case of Stephen (Acts 6 and 7).

A fourth aspect– combining the first and third– is peacemaking, which is especially relevant to the twenty-first century.

### b. The basis
The basis of lay priesthood is found in Peter's first epistle: 'Ye also, as lively stones, are built up a spiritual house, an holy priesthood, to offer up spiritual sacrifices, acceptable to God by Jesus Christ' (1 Peter 2:5 AV) and, 'You are a chosen people, a royal priesthood, a holy nation; a people belonging to God, that you may declare the the praises of him who called you' (1 Peter 2:9 NIV).

This chapter of the book is anecdotal and does not discuss the theology of bishops, priests and deacons. It suggests that there is a case for the Church of England to add a further category of priesthood– the unordained lay priest.

The word priest is used in this chapter to mean someone whose heart's desire is to help people to relate to God through Jesus Christ ever more deeply, and, as a matter of priority, to play their part in the coming of God's Kingdom on earth, here and now.

The means at the priest's disposal include the ministry of sacrament as well as word, the power of prayer, and essentially the impact of a loving and godly life that attempts to follow Christ and that is strategically directed, with wisdom and sensitivity.

In reflecting on the above four main aspects of lay priesthood, some awareness develops as to whether they are predominantly ministries of the Kingdom or ministries of the Church. First let us consider the process of seeking and finding that Kingdom, about which our Lord was always speaking.

### 1. GOD'S KINGDOM ON EARTH

#### a. Seeking and finding the Kingdom
Seek ye first the kingdom of God and his righteousness.

*Matthew 6:33 AV*

The first priority for followers of Christ is to search for situations where the Kingdom of God can be found. It is not enough to watch passively for his Kingdom, however intensively. We must actively look for it, deeply desire it, and question where it may be found, or how it may be induced.

The Kingdom is often discovered unexpectedly. Whereas you expect to find it in the Church, it is very often found in the world, shining brightly like gold dust in black soil. Its beauty reflects the glory of God at the place where virtue has triumphed over the worldliness of men and women, if only to a limited extent. Recognising the Kingdom is itself a gift, because it is often hidden.

> The kingdom of heaven is like treasure hidden in a field. When a man found it, he hid it again, and then in his joy went and sold all he had and bought that field. Matthew 13:44 NIV

The kingdom of heaven is like virtue hidden in a trading company. When a man found it, he did not separate it from its context and environment but left it where it was. He got excited by what he had seen, sold all that he had and bought the company. Then he developed it by directing the love of God to work upon the virtues and gifts that had been all but smothered, thus nurturing the once-hidden treasure in its own surroundings, which have the potential to be enriched.

The formation of Traidcraft, instigated by Richard Adams, Brian Hutchins and others, had some similarities to this. In the case of Traidcraft[1] the field was trade; the hidden treasure that was found was the humble, suffering poor on whom God's blessing rests, and their ability to produce quality goods. Their need was for a system of fair trade, replacing exploitation by rich middlemen with justice and righteousness, regardless of whether the beneficiaries were Christians or not– the love of God being for all humanity. Supplying these needs has provided a demanding and fulfilling ministry for many dedicated lay people. It is essentially a Kingdom work led by Christian people, rather than a Church work; more a service ministry than an exercise of priesthood; Christianisation rather than evangelism. Evangelism is in obedience to the second great commission to preach the gospel (Matthew 28:19; Mark 16:15):

Christianisation is in obedience to the first great commission to take responsibility for God's creation (Genesis 1:26, 28); in the light of Christ, in the power of the Holy Spirit and with a vision of God's Kingdom coming on earth.

The layman may need to move from ministry to priesthood as he develops the treasure. For this Kingdom work he needs support and encouragement from the Church, advice when he asks for it, but not interference! Least of all does he need to be uprooted and ordained into the Church as an NSM or OLM, etc. It is *unordained Kingdom priesthood* that is needed. Being a servant ( *diakonos*: deacon, minister or servant) was Stephen's starting point, but he moved on to priesthood while continuing to serve at tables. In the Church of England a deacon does not usually have to prove his humility as a servant before he is priested almost automatically, after a year or two. The *unordained Kingdom priest* is by contrast the one who, with the support of colleagues and led by the Holy Spirit, begins to minister the word and sacrament in the place where he continues to serve. This may happen with or without the encouragement of the Church of England– hopefully with!

### b. Growth of the Kingdom

Traidcraft's original hope of being like a tiny grain of mustard seed (Matthew 13: 31-32), with a Christianising effect on the marketplace, has been far exceeded. Several similar groups have sprung up, public awareness has been raised and public opinion influenced by their perseverance in the cause of fair trade for developing world producers. Some goods, which twenty years ago were largely stored in people's garages for coffee morning sales, are now selling well in supermarkets. Traidcraft is now a consultant on fair trade to Gerber on fruit juice, and to Waitrose on wine. The turnover of Traidcraft is approaching £11 million p.a., of which 27 per cent is from supermarkets. Further expansion is planned. Present capital (2002) is £1.8 million.

### c. Two fallacies about the Kingdom

The words 'Kingdom of heaven' and 'Kingdom of God' emphasise different aspects of the Kingdom. 'Kingdom of God' focuses on the Ruler of the Kingdom, the King to whose rule we are to submit as citizens of the Kingdom. On the other hand, heaven (*ouranos*), a spatial word, draws our attention to its territorial, yet unearthly, nature, its social as well as spiritual dimension. The Jews had a promised land as well as a God to rule them and it. For a comprehensive review of the Kingdom, see the writings of the new Bishop of Durham[2].

Those Christians who resist their responsibility towards society and for the whole creation say that the Kingdom is individual and merely internal and spiritual. For them, Luke 17:21 is best translated, 'The kingdom of God is within you' (NIV) but it can be translated 'among you' or 'between you', thus opening up the social and corporate aspects of the Kingdom.

The nature of God's Kingdom coming on earth as in heaven is partial and transient, appearing and disappearing, but glimpsed at least. We have discovered that this is particularly so in peacemaking (see section 6).

## 2. CHURCH, KINGDOM AND WORLD

The lead concept for the Kingdom is contained in the Lord's Prayer. We pray to our Father in heaven: 'Thy kingdom come on earth as it is in heaven', and conclude, 'Thine is the kingdom.' The Kingdom is primarily the Father's, just as the creation is primarily his, and he is the person of the Godhead most central in it. It is therefore not surprising that Christians and non-Christians work together, and members of different Churches cooperate better, in Kingdom projects in God's creation than in Church projects. This cooperation is helped by the fact that all love in the world is from God (1 John 4:7), and is found in varying degrees in all who are made in the image of God, however spoiled. Christians do not have the monopoly on love, though love is maximised in Christ as we apply it and follow Him. In Kingdom work, where love is central and essential, both Christians and non-Christians are channels of God's love and work together in His creation. *The circle of love is wider than the circle of faith.*

By contrast, the fundamental basis for Church work is in a shared faith in Christ. The incarnate Son of God, Jesus Christ, is the central person in the Church and its Head (Ephesians 1:22, etc.). *Faith is the basis, whereas love is the greatest* (1 Corinthians 13:13).

Kingdom work seeks an alternative society The New Testament never speaks of 'building' the Kingdom, even in England's green and pleasant land! It is more a question of praying for it, seeking, finding, unlocking, entering, and catching glimpses of it. By contrast, it can be said that the Church is built (Matthew 16:18). It is a worshipping, believing body of people, who look to Christ for their salvation, and eternal life.

It is possible to disagree with almost any statement distinguishing Church from Kingdom, because they overlap, and most truth lies in the overlap. Nevertheless there are differences, as also between Kingdom priesthood and Church priesthood. Anglican clergy are neither selected nor trained for Kingdom work. They have their hands full sustaining the Church.

### a. Church and world
In the Church of England, Church work as we normally think of it is centred on one or more buildings and overseen or led by an ordained priest, who, put simplistically, conducts services, pastors those who attend and evangelises those who do not. In an evangelising mode, obedient to the second great commission, the Church is calling people to repent and believe in Christ (Acts 2:38; 16:31), to become cleansed from worldliness, and to be separate (2 Corinthians 6:17).

### b. Church and Kingdom
The Church, which holds the keys of the Kingdom (Matthew 16:19), passes on the power to unlock the doors of the world and to introduce Christian ideas and methods. In a Christianising mode, obedient to the first great com-mission, the Church equips its members to be in the world though not of the world (John 17:11, 14, 15, 16, 18) doing good work. Kingdom workers, relate to the world with a different emphasis from Church workers, identify-ing with it rather than contrasting to it.

Whereas 'the Kingdom of heaven has suffered violence, and the violent take it by force' (Matthew 11:12 NRSV) , the 'gates of hell shall not prevail against' the Church of Jesus Christ (Matthew 16:18 AV). When a Kingdom project crashes, it is as well that the Church is around to take care of any who may get hurt in the process. Those engaged mostly in Kingdom work need the Church for anchorage and sometimes for refuge, but their deepest fellowship will be with like-minded workers, developing Kingdom priesthood.

### c. Kingdom and world

In politics, the Christian Socialist Movement (CSM) and the Conservative Christian Fellowship, Christian MPs, bishops and others in the House of Lords, play their part in bringing Christian principles to bear in formulating policies. Non-Christian pressure groups may be in sympathy, and cooperation with them is valuable, as was exemplified by John Stuart Mill's association with CSM. In recent years much noble work has been done in struggling with the moral issues of our times, Christians and those of other faiths, and none, often working together.

Sometimes new institutions such as schools or hospitals, or more controversially trade unions, have been introduced to society by Christians, and have chapels or chaplaincies.

In the field of psychiatry, the outstanding work of people such as Dr Frank Lake[3] and Dr Kenneth McAll[4] needs to be continued by an increasing number of clergy and laity. Both were laymen. Incidentally, Kenneth McAll frequently presided at the Holy Communion, which was central to his whole new ministry of 'healing the family tree'. Frank Lake transformed the ability of bishops to handle the difficult cases amongst their clergy and raised the standard of pastoral care and psychological understanding throughout the Church.

In most places of work deeds speak louder than words (Matthew 7:16). Where Christians produce good quality work that improves their company, a Christian fellowship, a 'Kingdom' group, an office or factory church, may result.

### d. Church, Kingdom and world

Large, vigorous, broadminded Anglican churches can bring together all these elements. Ichthus is a good example of a House Church which does so.

### 3. THE KINGDOM IN COMMERCE AND INDUSTRY

From the experience of Christian Industrial Enterprises Ltd (CIEL) two examples may ring bells for those who have dedicated their lives to increasing the influence of Christianity in commerce and industry. The examples come from Pilkingtons,who make glass in St Helens, Lancashire, and from Plessey Electrical.

Early in his career, David Pilkington had started a Christian Union within Pilkingtons. However, as he gained promotion he found that the CU meetings were not directly relevant to the company or stimulating to his work as a director. When the company had a major strike it was a quite different Christian body that proved relevant. In 1958 Tom Chapman had been elected as Divisional Organiser AEUW for North London, defeating the Communist candidate by a single vote[5]. Two years later the Communists made sure that he was the one to be ousted. From 1960, working with the Board of Social Responsibility of the Church of England, Tom formed a network of groups all over the country, made up of any who opposed extreme left-wing activity in industry. A few went to St Helens, Lancashire, listened at grassroots' level, gained access to Pilkingtons Board of Directors through David, and advised what offer the Board should make[6]. They followed this advice and made the offer, which was accepted. The strike was over.

CIEL was in touch with two Plessey CUs, one in Southampton and one in Nottingham. The Southampton CU adhered to the same 'basic evangelical agenda' as the Pilkington CU– prayer and Bible study, personal witness and evangelism, repentance, salvation and justification by faith. At Beeston in Nottingham, however, they had moved on (Hebrews 6:1) seeing the point of being relevant to the concerns of the company, and praying for problems that were affecting its well-being. In some cases management and trade unions had actually asked them to pray, and real answers to prayer had resulted. At the time when CIEL was in touch one department of Plessey Telecoms, with about 600 employees, was in danger of being closed down for lack of orders. One of the Sales Reps, a member of the CU, was sent out to the Far East, while the other members prayed for new business and that the threatened department would not have to close. The whole site seemed to be aware of this prayer focus. Three weeks later, they heard that the CU member had received orders approaching £2 million worth of business, including one order that would keep the threatened department going for up to a year.

On a very much smaller scale, inspired partly by Fritz Schumacher[7], CIEL was active in encouraging Christians to form Christian companies, including Traidcraft. Establishing Traidcraft as a company, rather than a funded charity, enabled it to have a greater influence in the market place.

Roger Sawtell[8], chairman of Traidcraft for several years, was very active in encouraging the establishment of Christian co-operatives, especially The Daily Bread Co-operative, which still prospers. He was also instrumental in getting the Industrial Common Ownership Act, 1976, on to the statute book.

CIEL was also influenced by Scott Bader Ltd, where Ernest Bader gave his shares to create the Scott Bader Commonwealth. Common ownership transformed the spirit of the company. More thought needs to be given to the ways in which the Holy Spirit transforms the esprit de corps of a company or community.

Another Christian who showed inspiring and energetic leadership was George Goyder, executive chairman of British International Paper, who stressed the importance of the need to extend membership of the company to the employees, and also of consulting consumers, suppliers and the local community. 'Means must be found to measure the company's social as well as financial performance,' he wrote in one of his influential books[9].

To what extent will Christians take up the issue of social audit in major companies ? In India, Ghandi's theory of trusteeship– that the wealthy should act as trustees of their possessions and power– had some influence on industry. For example, the TATA group of companies have undertaken social audits since 1980[10] and British American Tobacco have published (2002) their first Social Report, in which the Rt Revd Dr David Jenkins and the Revd Dr Charles Yeats of Durham Ethics were involved as UK Dialogue Moderator and Facilitator respectively. This provides an interesting example of the involvement of ordained clergy in industry, more often seen in the work of industrial missioners.

An important initiative in relating theology to organisational and other structures is the work of Christian Schumacher[11]. He has successfully demonstrated with many practical examples, how the doctrines of the Trinity, the creeds and the sacraments within the Church can provide a supreme exemplar for the design of corporate organisations and work places in industry, health services and central Government. When work is theologically grounded, it is made 'whole' in terms of effectiveness, motivation of those involved, environmental responsibility, sustainable development and spiritual significance– the birth pangs of the new creation.

Apart from the Christian Unions, several bodies provide Christian fellowship in industry and commerce. The Industrial Christian Fellowship (ICF) gives the lead in widening the agenda to a broader concern for the company as a whole, for which the stories from Pilkingtons and Plessey indicate a need. It provides fellowship for Christians who take their responsibility for industry seriously, under the first great commission. ICF have also produced a very interesting series of fifty or so pamphlets[12].

A further strategic point needs consideration. When making bread, the correct proportions of yeast to dough are vital. So it is in the Christianisation of a company: a sufficiently high proportion of Christians is needed, to act as 'yeast' (Matthew 13:33). There is tremendous potential for ministry and even lay priesthood in industry and commerce, but the Kingdom will not appear in a company without the right proportions. There is an opportunity for Christians to focus on working in selected companies in sufficient numbers to become the leaven which can Christianise the whole company. The life-giving contribution that Christianity can make contrasts strikingly with what can be the deadening contribution of 'political correctness', bureaucracy or authoritarianism.

## 4. LAY PRIESTHOOD IN THE PARISH

Fifty years ago, the laity in the Church of England was important for cleaning the brass and arranging the flowers, but nowadays the laity also preach and lead services. Fifty years on, laymen may be used to regularly and consecrate at Holy Communion. It is already happening more than is usually realised.

Interregnums provide the best insight into the capabilities of the laity. A thousand stories could be told of times when groups of lay people have led their churches into expansion, or at least sustained the congregation. It is important that a few of the stories be told so that conclusions may be drawn about the present ability and future potential of the laity.

The interregnum in our parish of Bix within a small benefice lasted nine months, and the congregation held steady, or increased very marginally. Outside clergy came in twice a month to take Communion services. There were contingency plans for baptisms, weddings and funerals. Bix already had three members who preached regularly, brought on by the far-sighted retiring rector. There were several willing to lead the prayers. From these we trained three to lead services. Crucially, we had a churchwarden who took a lot of trouble ensuring that everybody was happy, in church and village. Bix did not have any lay readers, licensed lay preachers, NSMs, OLMs, or house-for-duty clergy. During the interregnum, the team, which was virtually the whole church congregation, jelled together exceptionally well. The whole infrastructure grew together in mutual respect and friendship (Ephesians 4:16), strengthened by integration and support from the whole village.

The only thing that was done differently during this time was the issuing of a 'thought for the month', which we put through the letter box of every house in the three villages that made up the parish. Everybody helped with this, and discovered something about the priesthood of all believers within themselves, towards the Church, and especially towards the village.

The programme was comfortably sustained for those nine months. Moreover, had it been Anglican policy to allow lay presidency at Holy Communion, there were one or two of our ex-churchwardens and elder statesmen who could have performed the rôle acceptably and grown spiritually in the process. Church policy, however, denies this growth opportunity to lay people, though it is not clear that there is any scriptural basis for doing so. In time, could a benefice team have been created to take baptisms, weddings and funerals in an acceptable way? Diocesan training for that could be helpful. All Churches accept that a lay person can baptise; that the couple are the priests at a church wedding; and that there is no objection to laity taking funerals.

Church plants that take place in central London and elsewhere are, of course, led by ordained clergy but also develop a huge amount of lay ministry, as do Alpha courses, including lay ministry of the word, but not yet of the sacrament.

### Ordained and unordained priesthood

Perhaps some thought should be given to the difference between ordained and unordained priests in the Church. An ordained priest is normally full-time and paid, has been carefully selected, trained for at least two years, and ordained by the bishop, into one denomination only, that is, the Church of England. Called Reverend, clothed in dog collars and robed in church, with career structures ahead, ordained priests are sometimes thought of as the officers of the Church, whereas in reality they are more like its officials, similar to civil servants– the old title 'Clerk in Holy Orders' is more appropriate. Most would do better operating with a lay chairman from the parish. Much of the attitude that ranks clergy so definitively above laity dates back to the days when only the clergy could read and write !

An unordained lay priest in the Church has the same desire as an ordained priest to relate people to Christ. His desire to develop the Kingdom may be greater. Unencumbered by church structure, uniform or career prospects, the laity are freer. They are often knowledgeable about the Bible but not theologically trained; free agents, independent of church funds but strongly influenced by church colleagues and other Christian supporters. Their time commitment to the parish may vary from year to year: one vicar may be enthusiastic about their contribution; the next may sideline them. Their experience of life, general and specialised knowledge, and feel for the neighbourhood may be exceptionally valuable. Their suitability for the work will have emerged slowly and been observed by other members of the church.

Where the parish is a social unit, attempts to join with other churches in a benefice do not work well. Even when the congregation drops to twenty or the church building needs heavy expenditure, it will therefore still be desirable to have weekly worship in the parish. One possibility is to hand back the property to the diocese for redevelopment, and contract out of the diocesan quota. A Church of England house church, organised and led by laity, could then be established and the expense of clergy saved. The redeveloped church property should consider providing space for Christian charitable work. The right time to change to a house church may have been reached when most of the available energy of church members is used up in maintaining the church, and there is little left for outward looking service to the community and for evangelism– possibly when numbers have dropped to between thirty and twenty.

The clear transfer of responsibility to the laity will in itself contribute to dynamic change.

## 5. CHARITABLE WORK

One of the most inspiring experiences in life is seeing those in need receiving the love they require. To be involved as a channel of such love and to find the inner resources to respond is, of course, even more uplifting. It is often done well by humanitarian charities but when combined with an awareness of channelling God's love, maximised in Christ, to people overcome by sickness, suffering and sin, we glimpse his redemption of the world and the glory of God. Those who make such work into a career are exercising a loving priesthood, suffering with those who suffer. They are mostly lay people and many of the best are women.

Perhaps the most demanding work of all is with physically or mentally handicapped people. Almost as demanding is the work of the Langley House Trust, which cares for men and women who are homeless on leaving prison. This work is particularly relevant now, with hard-to-place offenders being one of the Home Office's greatest difficulties. The rehabilitation of sex offenders and violent offenders, while protecting the public, presents special problems. The due process of criminal law is a 'schoolmaster' (Galatians 3:24 AV) whose punishment brings the offender so low that he instinctively looks in new directions for restoration. The joy of newness of life (2 Corinthians 5:17) results from finding the love of Christ through Christians who visit him in prison and offer rehabilitation afterwards in a house enriched by some understanding of how to overcome sin through the death of Christ and his forgiveness experienced daily.

A government report in the 1960s singled out Langley House Trust as the best model of aftercare for men leaving prison. Langley became a tremendous Christian witness to Government. The Home Office started funding Langley House Trust and made very few conditions, having the wisdom to realise that Langley knew how to operate. They had spotted the vital fact that men resident at a Langley House, run as a home with prayer and with live-in caring staff, virtually never re-offended. This was to the Home Office a pearl of great price and they were careful not to crush it, since any decrease in re-offending was a major budget saving.

You will seldom meet more dedicated Christians than the splendid people who do this work in the Langley Houses 24 hours a day, 365 days a year. Their heart's desire is to apply the gospel of Jesus Christ in practical ways, for each individual under their care, and restore them to fulness of life. Here the laity may experience direct empowerment by the Holy Spirit for their work with the ex-offenders and others, communicating the gospel of love mainly by life and by deed.

The trustees and management have the primary responsibility for sustaining and developing their staff's capacity for this ministry and priesthood: their spiritual development cannot be taken for granted. Staff need support and encouragement in their work with such a difficult client group. Indeed, their zeal can be dampened by administrative demands, excessive interference by Government and other funders, which become ways of quenching the Spirit, (1 Thessalonians 5:19), undermining the high quality of service and shortening the length of service of which the person is capable.

To develop this type of priesthood is a responsibility as well as a privilege for the Church. To maximise the effectiveness of such representatives of Christ throughout the world of charities, it may be appropriate to develop their knowledge of the Bible beyond the basic evangelical agenda. The right to celebrate the Eucharist will also sometimes be more appropriate than bringing in outsiders. If the experience of the Langley House Trust is anything to go by, the Church of England is sometimes outshone by other Churches in producing house staff capable of sustaining the high level of love that is demanded by this sort of work. The pastoral task of inducing compassion in souls presents a real challenge.

## 6. PEACEMAKING

Peacemaking is worth a special mention because it is the only New Testament ministry (2 Corinthians 5:18) that is attached to a Beatitude (Matthew 5:9) and because today's world highlights the need for peacemakers. There are many forms of Christian peacemaking. This section focuses mainly on the work of CHIPS (Christian International Peace Service).

Every parish of the Church of England prays for peace every Sunday, the 1948 Lambeth Conference chose reconciliation as its main theme, and peace is high on the agenda of the Archbishop of Canterbury. Jesus Christ is our peace (Ephesians 2:14), individually and corporately. He has made peace not only between God and humanity, but also between Gentiles and Jews (Ephesians 2:11-18), whom God had separated when he called out Abraham. Roman Gentiles destroyed Jerusalem in AD 70 and the Jews, with a lot of US support, are destroying the Palestinians in our time. Nevertheless, we affirm that Jesus Christ is our peace, who has made peace between Jews and Gentiles and between other ethnic groupings. We have to make Christ's peace real, and make sense of all the contradictions, working amongst paradox. It has to be realised also that wars and rumours of wars will continue until the end of time (Matthew 24:6), and that only in eternity will the lion lie down with the lamb (Isaiah 11:6), but that does not mean that we should be lukewarm in taking up this ministry.

CHIPS started its work in Cyprus from 1964 -1972 with a resident team. From 1967 to 1971, at a time when the Greek Cypriot government was having great difficulty in persuading Turkish Cypriots to resettle their villages, a small team of Christians, initiated by Michael Kennedy, resettled the Turkish Cypriot village of Kidasi, Paphos, in a predominantly Greek Cypriot area. This is another example of Christians being able to do certain jobs that governments cannot do.

In 1974, Turkey invaded Cyprus. At Kidasi, a Turkish Cypriot shepherd's wife was waylaid in the fields. Her head was severed from her body. Because of this and other incidents, all Turkish Cypriots fled northwards. Had the work of CHIPS been a waste of time? Ten years later, one Turkish Cypriot answered, 'You should be ashamed of yourself for asking that question. You won the hearts of the people and that should be enough for any man.' Others said, 'You gave us the best five years of our lives, back in our own houses, cultivating our own fields, sitting under our favourite trees, drinking coffee in our own village.'

In 1967 Mr Clerides and Mr Denktash, Greek and Turkish Cypriot political leaders, started talks; and continued talking until Mr Clerides retired in 2003. At the time of writing there is no settlement and not much hope of one, but we hope against hope.

If you can't have peace in the midst of war, conflict, and paradox, it is not the peace of Christ. The usual Greek word for peace, a word that means 'the absence of conflict', and also tranquillity and calm, is hardly ever used in the New Testament. The Greek word that is mostly used, eirene, means 'creative harmony'. This peace, the peace of Christ, is not limited to individual peace–peace in the heart. Jesus himself is our peace, but that peace has to be made real by examples of his Kingdom coming on earth, even if they appear and disappear. Peace has to be a corporate affair if it is to be relevant. These and other matters are much discussed in CHIPS seminars[13], which become more popular with every outbreak of violence in the world, and as people realise that there is a Christian ministry of peacemaking that needs to be developed.

These same tensions exist in the current CHIPS Project in NE Uganda among the Karimojong and Iteso tribes there. CHIPS started with a seed lending scheme, diversifying into water development, assisted by Christian Engineers in Development (CED), an excellent and very professional Christian initiative founded by Peter Stern.

In Uganda, followers of Christ, working for peace between two tribes, dug wells in villages that had a water shortage. The underground water was the hidden treasure exposed by CED. The spirit in which the wells were dug by the villagers themselves was important as is the fact that the water is shared with the enemy tribe. One of the villagers involved was a drunkard when CHIPS came to his area and encouraged him to join in the digging. When he began to ask, 'Who are these people and what is CHIPS?' a team member explained and also told him about Jesus. He became a Christian, gave up drinking and began a new life. When his community saw this dramatic change, they too began to turn to Christ, until the whole village of 250 people became 'newly born' and formed a 'church at the well' where they worship God, where his rule prevails and there is a love amongst them that had never existed before. They help the old and the poor and needy with their gardening and farming so that they will have food, and they allow the enemy tribe to use the well. The drunkard had become a priest.

### Lomaratoit

In 1997, CHIPS in NE Uganda decided to set up a new base nearer a place called Iriri, which was a major centre of tension. The Karimojong tribesmen with their spears and guns and scanty clothing may not have looked very intelligent to the Western eye, but appearances can be deceptive. They knew that they wanted CHIPS to be situated near a borehole that was a place of ambush, a place of wild animals and a place for robbers. Even they were terrified of this evil place called Lomaratoit. The Iteso agreed. Both realised that this area, that had not been inhabited in living memory, had agricultural potential.

The CHIPS team found the courage in Christ to build houses there and move to Lomaratoit. It was hoped that some few Iteso and Karamojong would settle in the area and find the ability to co-operate together. But it was not a few who came. During the next three years 3,500 came and established a viable economic and social unit. It was particularly remarkable that the area attracted many Karimojong who wanted to give up the use of guns and their itinerant cattle herding and become settled farmers, living at peace with the Iteso people. They even wanted to send their children to school. Providentially, a retired schoolmaster offered his services. We erected a sheltered place and soon a hundred children were attending regularly. This Karimojong settlement caught a glimpse of the Kingdom.

On the evening of 14 January 2001, the Ugandan Army (UPDF) arrived at Lomaratoit and opened fire, killing ten people including a CHIPS worker. They forced the CHIPS team to leave. Nobody knows why it happened. All the settlers abandoned the area. At a single stroke, in a few minutes, the UPDF not only destroyed the work of years, they destroyed a viable potential for peace. To some degree the Kingdom of heaven had come to Lomaratoit, but the violent took it by force (Matthew 11:12). The consequent court martial seems to have been suppressed and all the culprits released without punishment.

In the midst of all this, despite the danger, the CHIPS team move in and out, providing agricultural, veterinary and water development services. Life is very difficult for them. It is not easy not to be afraid. The CHIPS presence, amazingly, has encouraged some of the settlers to return again to the border area, and CHIPS have provided them with seed, and other help in the midst of trouble. This year (2003) the school will be rebuilt by the government on a less vulnerable site.

## 7. THE LAY CELEBRATION OF HOLY COMMUNION

If a lay person is to move from ministry to priesthood, he or she will need to be able to use the word of God and feel free to minister the Eucharist. Alwyn Marriage in an excellent book on the ministry of the laity[14], tells how the lay presidency of the Eucharist was established in the house group of which she was a member.

At Kidasi in Cyprus, the CHIPS team there invited ordained Anglicans to come and give us Holy Communion because we attached importance to the sacrament as an essential part of our life and work. The priest who brought matters to a head was a Forces chaplain who refused to pray for any head of state other than those mentioned in the Church of England Prayer Book–though he had been told that the service would be attended by volunteers from many nationalities and from different Churches. He was particularly asked to pray for the Governments of the countries represented. This he refused to do. After further remonstration and discussion, he was asked at least to pray for Archbishop Makarios, President of Cyprus, and for Dr Kuchuk, the Turkish Cypriot Vice President. He said he could not do this because he was paid by the Church of England and could only pray as stipulated in the Prayer Book for the royal family and the British Government.

We had no building large enough to hold all our expanded summer teams, so owe would put out chairs in the rough road that ran past our houses and formed part of the village street. Among the students there was always a vigorous sense of worship and on one occasion their singing attracted shepherds from the neighbourhood. By the time we reached the moment for Communion there was a Greek Cypriot shepherd on one side of the congregation with his flock of sheep and on the other a Turkish Cypriot shepherd with his sheep and goats. At the time of Communion, some did not partake.

Next day I visited the nearby Turkish Cypriot village of Aghios Georgios and sat down at the coffee shop to talk with others who were there resting from the hot August sun under the shade of a vine. In Cyprus the shepherds were considered to be amongst the least educated and most ignorant of people. I was particularly glad that the Turkish Cypriot shepherd who had attended our worship the previous day sat down next to me. I was looking forward to a conversation with a Muslim about Christian worship. The heart of the conversation went something like this:

'I noticed yesterday that when most of you went forward some stayed in their seats,' said the shepherd.

'Yes.'

'Why was that?'

'Perhaps there were a few who did not feel ready to take part fully that day.'

'Or,' asked the shepherd, 'perhaps they were Roman Catholics who did not want to share with Protestants?'

'Perhaps,' I responded rather limply.

There then followed some deserved comments about peacemakers who were not at peace amongst themselves. How could CHIPS expect Greek and Turkish Cypriots who were of completely different religions to be sharing together as one, if CHIPS who were all Christians could not share together?

In those days, on the way to and from Cyprus it was possible to visit the World Council of Churches in Geneva, the Vatican in Rome and the Patriarch of the Orthodox Church in Istanbul. These were the years of good Pope John XX111's Vatican Council and its aftermath.

One of the offices that received me was the Secretariat for Christian Unity. I thought it would be reasonable to ask for a ruling that Roman Catholics should be allowed to participate fully in CHIPS Eucharists. I entered their offices with a fair head of steam, whether driven by the power of the Holy Spirit or by sinful anger, I will never be quite sure. What is sure is that the priests of the Secretariat dealt with the situation with quiet vision and generosity of spirit. The one with whom I met considered that the incident that had occurred in Cyprus was a scandal and that Roman Catholics who joined our team should feel free to participate fully in the CHIPS celebration of the sacrament of Holy Communion, or, alternatively, that an opportunity should be provided in the service for Roman Catholics to apologise for not receiving and to explain that the rules of their Church, with which they disagreed, did not permit them to do so.

In the Secretariat they had come to the conclusion that the leader of groups such as CHIPS should normally be the celebrant, not an outsider. Their thinking was that if the Holy Spirit had raised up such a work under the leadership of a layman, then he should be the one to accept with humility the responsibility of celebrating the death of Christ, subject to the consent of the team. He therefore urged me, as team leader, to preside at the service, including the consecration of the elements.

Back home I discussed the question with many Anglican clergy from different persuasions and of different schools of thought. Almost all of them responded in the same way. They saw no objection, biblical or theological, to the lay celebration of the Eucharist, but they did not want to be asked, as they would have to refer it to the bishop and the bishops were agreed not to sanction lay celebration. Almost all of them said, 'Don't ask me, just go ahead and do it.' In fact, some argued that Holy Communion, like the Passover, should be celebrated in the home by the head of the family and should never have been uprooted and moved into the church.

If the Church of England ever wanted to allow the lay presidency of Holy Communion at parish level, a start could be made with those who have served the church faithfully and are held in respect by the people. Perhaps house group leaders could also be encouraged to lead Communion services with their group. It would be sad if the inflexibility that was unable to accommodate the House Church movement within the Church of England remains unable to welcome new patterns.

This chapter is not about the various new forms of ordained priesthood that the Church of England is developing with refreshing imagination, such as NSM, LOM, etc. It is about the potential for an unordained priesthood. As far as parish work is concerned, there should not be any special management difficulties in giving some laity, selected by the people and approved by the hierarchy, the right to preside at the Eucharist. Extended Communion is unsatisfactory. Chairing the PCC and some other tasks normally carried out by the clergy could also be handed over to laity.

It may be more difficult to decide how to manage the presidency of the Eucharist in Christian charitable work or in the Christianising of industry and commerce and the secular world in general. Perhaps a non-diocesan bishop could be given the responsibility to oversee this development.

## 8. CONCLUSIONS

What can the Church of England do to develop unordained lay priesthood?

The Church hierarchy has a great opportunity to develop the potential of the laity. It has been clever in developing lay potential by creating lengthy interregnums and by allowing church plants. There is an opportunity now to take things to their logical conclusion in developing lay leadership in the Church, by developing lay training, by authorising lay presidency of the Eucharist and by giving the laity responsibility for small congregations.

The greatest potential for lay priesthood, however, lies beyond the church in the narrow parochial and diocesan sense of the word. The priesthood of all believers is a royal priesthood (1 Peter 2:9) because it is primarily a priesthood of the Kingdom rather than of the Church. A great virtue of the Church of England is its deep integration into British society and culture. It is essentially British and is therefore in a strong position to make a good contribution to the Christianisation of secular life in the UK and to the well-being of the nation.

The astonishing amount of charitable work in the UK reflects the best of our national character. In this Anglicans play a full part. There are now many situations in which the role of the laity in charitable work is ripe for development from service and ministry to priesthood.

---

**Notes**

[1] See Richard Adams, *Who Profits*, Lion, 1989.

[2] Tim Wright, *Jesus and the Victory of God*, SPCK, 1996, chs 6-10, and *The Challenge of Jesus*, SPCK, 2000.

[3] See Frank Lake, *Clinical Theology*, DLT, 1966.

[4] Kenneth McAll, *Healing the Family Tree*, Sheldon Press, 1986.

[5] See the forthcoming biography for details: David Pilkington, *A Promise Kept*, Shepheard Walwyn Publishers Ltd., to be published summer 2003.

[6] David Pilkington, *The Pilkington Srike*, unpublished, available from the author.

[7] E. F. Schumacher, *Small is Beautiful*, first published in Great Britain by Blond & Briggs, 1963, Abacus Books, 1974, 1992, etc.

[8] Author of *The Church that Meets in Your House*, and *A Simple Communion*, both available from Daily Bread Co-operative, The Old Laundry, Bedford Road, Northampton NN4 7AD.

[9] George Goyder, *The Responsible Worker*, Hutchinson, 1975, p.111; also see The Responsible Company, Hutchinson, c. 1965.

[10] Social Audit Committee Report, Tata Press Ltd., Bombay, August 1980.

[11] Christian Schumacher, *God in Work: Discovering the divine pattern for work in the new millennium*, Lion, 1998.

[12] ICF Theme Pamphlets, published 1980s, from the Industrial Christian Fellowship, St Matthews House, 100 George Street, Croydon.

[13] See also, Keith Lindsey, *Making Peace: Biblical principles and the experience of CHIPS*, 2002, available from CHIPS, Bix Bottom Farm, Henley-on-Thames, RG9 6BH.

[14] Alwyn Marriage, *The People of God*, DLT, 1995.

# 17. Leadership for a new generation

## MARK MILLS-POWELL

Given the possibility of ecumenical bad practice, does the concept of the whistle-blower make a positive or a negative contribution to the debate on change?

In relation to the pastoral ministry of care and oversight, does our insistence on traditional roles and structures deny us the opportunity for true experimentation?

*Mark Mills-Powell became Team Rector of the Linton Team Ministry (in the Diocese of Ely) in 2002. He previously served for eight years in the Diocese of Washington DC– a city that remains close to his heart. He wrote the Grove Booklet, Praying in the Shadow of the Bomb, when a curate in Liverpool.*

*In this chapter he argues that the episcopal ministry must become apostolic again.*

> The gifts he gave were that some would be apostles, some prophets, some evangelists, some prophets and teachers, to equip the saints for the work of the ministry, for building up the body of Christ, until all of us come to the unity of the faith and of the knowledge of the Son of God, to maturity, to the measure of the full stature of Christ.
>
> *Ephesians 4:11-13 NRSV*

That the Church of England is in decline, and suffering from a critical shortage of financial resources and stipendiary clergy, is now becoming indisputable, and that the leadership of an organisation should be held accountable for its performances goes without saying in most contexts. But in our situation there is an unwritten rule not to be too critical of those in positions of responsibility – at least not openly. For one thing, criticism will destroy your chances of promotion, and for another, it gives the impression of a lack of humility, meekness and submissiveness. The result is that sicknesses in the body are left to fester; while people in positions of power become more and more expert in managing decline.

### The apostolic ministry

But there are both contemporary examples and many illustrations from the early centuries of the Church's episcopal ministry being exactly what it is called to be: a genuinely apostolic function of the Body of Christ. The primitive Christian communities were cared for by one or several ministers, called either bishop or presbyter; only eventually did the pattern emerge of one minister, called a bishop, being responsible for one local church or diocese. The deacon was probably the earliest assistant minister and ranked high in relation to the bishop. Presbyters, as distinct from bishops, are met with for the first time in large towns or cities such as Antioch or Rome.

The problem for the Christian Church in large conurbations was how to provide for a scattered and growing Christian population that could no longer be accommodated under one roof, even had a suitable building become available. It is as representative of the bishop, therefore, that the second order of ministry, now called presbyter, first appears. Presbyters in the early Church were very much 'bishop's men' and felt themselves to be more part of an episcopal team than on permanent secondment to a parish. St Cyprian in the third century (addressing his presbyters) made a promise at the beginning of his episcopate that he would 'do nothing without your advice and the consent of the people'[1]. This was not exceptional. For many years, the town clergy in particular enjoyed privileged access to their bishop. They were his missioners and sat with him in the cathedral church. In effect, at that time, the norm was what Robert Brow (a scholar and experienced Anglican missionary statesman) advocates for today– apostles and mission teams functioning together. The bishop was rightly in the place of the apostle.

### The Christian community

In the 1970s, one Anglican bishop (Bill Frey, then Bishop of Colorado), under the influence of the Church of the Redeemer, Houston, Texas, experimented with a model that has certain resonances with this earlier pattern, except that the focus was not primarily on sharing life more deeply with ordained presbyters but rather with lay people. He opened up his home to make it available as a place for extended Christian community. One obvious advantage in such a situation is that another, who was sharing life with him closely, would be able to represent him faithfully in a place that he might not be able to attend.

Christian community, far from being an experiment that has failed in the life of the Church, is something that the Church simply cannot exist without. The only question is what forms of Christian community are most appropriate for what situations. Bishop Frey's experience in Denver, Colorado, and the normative experience of the Christian Church in the third century, and one could add the normative experience of the Celtic Christian missionary communities around their leader (bishop or abbot), all point in the same direction: to be effective in Christian mission and ministry there must be a significant depth to the experience of Christian koinonia. Christian service, ministry, and leadership develop most effectively when 'youngers' have the opportunity to rub shoulders with 'elders', know their heart, and model their behaviour.

### Christ's commission

In an age where fatherhood has been all but lost, there is a desperate need for spiritual fathers to be recognised and received. A good father does not use people; he invests in them, spends time with them, draws them out, sees their potential, and encourages them. It is tragic to meet so many people in the Church of Jesus Christ who feel they have been exploited and then discarded when convenient. Deep down, many people feel that they are appreciated and included only because of the needs they can meet and the uses they can fulfil for the leadership. Their acceptance is based on what they can do, and not on who they are. When their usefulness is gone, then so is the relationship. With this style of leadership, individuals end up feeling manipulated, hurt or angry. It seems that they can be jettisoned at a time of the leader's choosing. How many bishops or parish clergy have you experienced, who seem intent on manoeuvring their external circumstances apparently with the sole goal of enhancing their own personal power base? But such a way is so obviously antithetical to the way of Christ:

Who... did not regard equality with God as something to be exploited, but emptied himself, taking the form f a slave, being born in human likeness. And being found in human form, he humbled himself and became obedient to the point of death– even death on a cross.

*Philippians 2:6-8 NRSV*

Henri Nouwen, commenting on Jesus' commission to Peter, 'Feed my lambs . . .tend my sheep' (John 21:13, 16 NRSV), writes:

> Ministry is not only a communal experience, it is also a mutual experience. As Jesus ministers, so He wants us to minister. He wants Peter to feed His sheep and care for them, not as 'professional' who know their clients' problems and take care of them, but as vulnerable brothers and sisters, who know and are known, who care and are cared for, who forgive and are being forgiven, who love and are being loved . . . How can anyone lay down his life for those with whom he is not even allowed to enter into a deep personal relationship . . . We are not the healers, we are not the reconcilers, we are not the givers of life. We are sinful, broken, vulnerable people who need as much care as anyone we care for[2].

One of the most useful things I picked up during my formal training for ordination was the fact that we so often receive from the individuals we are called to minister to. As we open ourselves to become a channel of God's love for another, so again and again we receive love and are built up in the Holy Spirit. It's what people want more than anything else– authentic love. And when it is shared in the name of Christ, the Church's credibility soars. It is what people hope to find when they look to the Church. Tragically, all too often the inquirer or seeker may encounter the Church without seeing any significant depth of relationship or connectedness among its members. Additionally, it is possible to work for the Church as an ordained minister and experience much more Christian *koinonia* and support from one's local people than from other clergy.

### A system in crisis

All too often, the clergy experience their bishop or archdeacon as a somewhat distant figure, over-worked and distracted by a million other things, inaccessible and reluctant, or unable, to take an interest in one's work, concerns, or person. He represents a system that is more disabling than empowering– and a system seemingly worried that the whole edifice may be close to collapse. The nightmare scenario is for an individual to emerge (when one is trying as hard as one can to keep the show on the road), who has the audacity to proclaim, 'The Emperor has no clothes!'

But surely honesty and vulnerability would help. The vast majority of church folk are looking for Christian leaders who are truthful about the extent of the crisis facing the Church of England, and realistic about their own limitations and struggles as they seek to respond to it appropriately. Most people are not looking for messiah-figures who might try and pretend they can fix the problem, but rather people who will show genuine solidarity, be prepared to weep with those who weep and come alongside others with empathy and caring. Surely the good news of the Christian gospel is that we already have a Messiah, Jesus Christ, the righteous Lord of the Church, who is still looking for men and women who are honest about their shortcomings and failures and are therefore usable. We need to be reminded that not many of us Christian ministers and leaders 'were wise by human standards, not many were powerful, not many were of noble birth. But God chose what is foolish in the world to shame the wise; God chose what is weak in the world to shame the strong; God chose what is low and despised in the world, things that are not, to reduce to nothing things that are' (1 Corinthians 1:26-28 NRSV); and that when we are weak, then we are strong [2 Corinthians 12:10].

In his book *By What Authority?* William Barclay is at pains to emphasize that in the earliest stage of the Church's life bishops and presbyters were the same people. He quotes St Jerome: 'Among the ancients bishops and presbyters are the same, for the one is a term of dignity, the other of age.'[3] The distinction is that *presbuteros* describes the individual personally (normally an older person), while *episkopos* describes the individual from the point of view of the function performed (a function to oversee and superintend the flock of the Church. For example, in 1 Peter 5 elders (presbyters) are addressed, and in verse 2 they are urged to tend, *episkope*in, the flock. The duty of an elder or presbyter is to act as an *episkopos*. The pastoral ministry of care and oversight is essentially the same no matter who is exercising it: *it is meant to be a communication of the love and discernment of Jesus Christ, our Lord and Saviour.* This is the ministry that was in increasing demand when the Church had become established in so many towns and cities that the apostle and the apostolic team were no longer able to have first hand involvement with the new churches. This loving pastoral ministry has on the whole served the Western world well for over a thousand years.

### The apostolic ministry

The difficulty is that if the rapid decline of the Church is to be reversed, the Church in Western Europe needs the apostolic ministry far more urgently than any other form of ministry. As Robert Brow has written, 'The apostolic function is the most neglected and yet most necessary gift for the world-wide church.'4 The pastoral ministry is simply too blunt a tool to be able to make the impression that is needed in what have become essentially post-Christian societies. If the apostolic ministry is encouraged and given free reign, the style of the Christian Church will undoubtedly change significantly in the process because a serious attempt will be being made to reach people where they are rather than expecting them to make a cultural leap in order to gain access to a church.

The local pastor should not feel threatened by an increase in anointed and recognised apostolic ministry. Quite the reverse, it is very often exactly what he or she is looking for in encouragement, and fresh motivation. For myself, I can say I find it hard to imagine how I could have continued doing what I do without that sort of apostolic input, covering, love and inspiration. Similarly, it is my experience that when I and others have been invited to minister in other parishes or churches, our presence and contribution have seemed to be like water in a thirsty land. I wonder what percentage of the stipendiary clergy in the Church of England today are either hanging on by their finger nails, or have effectively given up and are just going through the motions. I fear that the proportion would be frighteningly high. A tragedy is that the bishop is often powerless to provide the sort of leadership to help in such situations. Perhaps trust has broken down between him and the local ordained pastor. Perhaps the ordained minister has become so isolated that he has given up on reaching out for help.

Often one-day courses are available that could help. Often counsellors or spiritual directors are around in the diocesan structure, who could provide some of the support and insight that could make a difference. It is quite unreasonable to expect one individual to meet all the needs. As Richard Hooker wrote, 'In some things every presbyter, in some things only bishops, in some things neither the one nor the other are the apostles' successors.'[5] The point is that whoever it comes from, apostolic leadership is the crying need of both clergy and laity alike; for the genuine apostle (or apostolic team) coming in from outside, by God's grace *ministers the Holy Spirit* into a situation that is in real need of fresh input.

The apostle has a burning vision for the Church as the holy Bride of Jesus Christ, that she is called to be. The apostle recognises that sometimes conventions will have to be disturbed in order for the Church to recover the holy self-esteem, that it has sometimes lost through neglect, abuse, or frequent put-downs. The apostle believes that all of God's people are being built together into a dwelling of God in the Holy Spirit:

> In him [Christ], the whole structure is joined together and grows into a holy temple in the Lord; in whom you [we] also are built together spiritually into a dwelling-place for God.
>
> *Ephesians 2:21 NRSV*

This is the vision that animates the apostle and he or she has confidence that it will be fulfilled, as Revelation 21.2f promises:

> I saw the holy city, the new Jerusalem, coming down out of heaven from God, prepared as a bride adorned for her husband. And I heard a loud voice from the throne saying, 'See, the home [tabernacle] of

God is among mortals. He will dwell with them; they will be his peoples, and God himself will be with them.'

*Revelation 21:2-3 NRSV*

Apostles have a sense of awe that Almighty God by his Holy Spirit desires to tabernacle in the Church in such a way, and that this is their true vocation and destiny. This reality relativises all other temporary and passing discouragements. The hope is renewed every time they are drawn into that mystical communion, in which they experience something of that future now, when they are so enabled to so delight in him that all their longing and desire feel satisfied and complete in him. Such an experience is tantalisingly alluded to by some lines of Fr Gilbert Shaw:

God, my heart is restless until it rests wholly in you.
Increase my faith that I may seek and find.
You are indeed a hidden God,
yet you reveal yourself in all your creatures.
You choose to be hidden within my heart,
the very Temple where You dwell,
revealing Yourself in the depth and height of my life...

In Your mercy, say within my soul, 'I am your salvation.'
My heart is open for you, say to my heart, 'I am your saving health.'
My heart is small and narrow, but come into it,
and by your coming enlarge it and dwell therein[6].

---

**Notes**

[1] Cyprian, *Epistola ad presbyteros et diaconos*, SPCK, 2001, pp. 5f.

[2] Henri Nouwen, *In the Name of Jesus: Reflections on Christian Leadership*, Crossroad, 1989, p.42.

[3] William Barclay, *By What Authority?*, Hodder & Stoughton, 1974.

[4] Quoted in David Pytches, *Leadership for New Life*, Hodder and Stoughton, 1998.

[5] David Pytches, op. cit.

[6] Fr Gilbert Shaw, *Seeds of Love*, SLG Press.

# 18. Liberating leaders for mission

## TREVOR BEESON

Trevor Beeson's plea for diocesan bishops to be granted 'time for reflection and strategic planning' alludes to the balance between faith and works; are there radical new approaches we may dare to embrace, through which each of us can meet our obligations, faced with internal down-sizing and external apathy?

It is in the nature of hierarchy that we accept the boundaries placed upon each tier of responsibility, irrespective of quality of delivery; should we be more vocal in testing, challenging, even subverting these– as a democratic right– in the quest for exemplars?

*Trevor Beeson, formerly the pioneering vicar of a new housing area in Stockton on Tees and later a canon of Westminster, Rector of St Margaret's, Westminster, and Chaplain of the House of Commons, is now Dean Emeritus of Winchester. Here he highlights (among other things) the crucial need for our leaders to be freed for prayerful reflection, the prerequisite for renewed and radical vision.*

Among the many valuable contributions to this volume, are the essay of Tim Dakin on mission, which demands and repays careful study, and the pleas for stronger episcopal and lay leadership, which seem to me to be specially important. There can be no revival of mission without visionary leadership.

The divine origin and mission of the Christian Church does not exempt it from the disciplines of organisation and, in common with secular institutions, it either sinks or swims according to the quality of those entrusted with its direction. That said, it must immediately be acknowledged that in every sphere of human activity leadership is exercised in many different ways. A dictatorship is said to be more successful than a sophisticated democracy in getting the trains to run on time, but the cost of such efficiency in terms of denial of human freedom and dignity in other parts of life is generally considered much too high to be acceptable.

Cruel twentieth-century experience has left no room for dictatorial leadership, though many examples of it remain, and although democracy produces many frustrations and disappointments it continues to be, as Winston Churchill famously said, the least bad form of government. Modern management in all areas also requires sensitive consultation and carefully structured devolution of responsibility if it is to be effective.

The Church's patterns of leadership and administration still owe much to the elementary forms discernible in the earliest days of its existence. These were, as one might expect of a first-century community, essentially patriarchal in character. This is not the place to revive the old debate about whether or not, and in what sense, today's bishops can be regarded as successors of the apostles chosen by Jesus to share in and continue his mission. But it is a fact that the patriarchal style of leadership expressed in an episcopal form of ministry, and handed on from age to age by the laying on of hands, has for almost 2,000 years been regarded as an integral element in the Catholic tradition of both East and West. Extended from the bishops to the members of the priesthood, it accords well with the concept of pastoral care displayed supremely by Jesus the Good Shepherd. It also provides the basis for the pioneering leadership necessary to dynamic missionary enterprise and reflects the personal character of the relationship between God and his people. At its best, episcopal ministry has been one of the Church's glories and been exercised by many saints; at its worst, it has been a source of shame and done irreparable harm to the Christian cause.

Throughout the twentieth century, the patriarchal concept of church leadership was challenged and in varying degrees, modified by the growing attachment to democracy in secular society. Much more powerful than this, however, was the emergence of biblical theology, which in turn led to a revival of the long-neglected understanding of the

Church as embracing the whole people of God. Such an understanding emphasises the importance of the ministry of every member, lay as well as ordained, and undermines any idea of privileged hierarchy. The liturgical movement has expressed this in the ordering of worship where, at the Eucharist, the priest is no longer the celebrant, but rather the president, and both the liturgy and the layout of the building are designed to emphasise the corporate character of the offering. Synodical government has brought shared decision-making at every level of the Church of England's life.

As long ago as 1952, Bishop Kenneth Kirk of Oxford, who was a good administrator as well as a much-loved pastor and a distinguished scholar, declared that the Church of England was faced with the almost impossible predicament of trying to combine patriarchal and democratic forms of government. This was before the advent of synodical government. Kirk did not regret episcopal involvement in administration and in a remarkable sermon, 'Beauty and Bands', preached at the consecration of his friend Glyn Simon as Bishop of Swansea and Brecon in 1954, he pointed out that much pastoral work is carried out or enabled by the bishop while he is involved in administration in his study.

Fifty years later, however, it would be interesting to have Kirk's comments on a *Church Times* report that in 1990 Archbishop George Carey spent three weeks presiding over the Lambeth Conference, visited 30 countries, delivered 140 sermons, speeches and addresses, made more than 50 broadcasts, contributed 10 articles to journals and books, spent many hours in the House of Lords and on other state affairs, gave innumerable interviews and dealt with a mountain of letters, emails and faxes. His car was equipped with a telephone and a computer to enable such work to be uninterrupted by journeys. He rose at 6.30 a.m. or earlier, rarely went to bed before midnight, and took one weekend off every six weeks.

The appointment in 2002 of Archbishop Rowan Williams as Dr Carey's successor was attended by almost universal praise. His combination of gifts– spiritual, intellectual, pastoral and the power of communication– make him a unique figure in Britain's religious life today. His accession to the throne of St Augustine at a moment when all the Churches are experiencing decline in numbers and low morale seems providential. There is great expectancy. But although some of the routine responsibilities of the archbishopric are to be delegated to other bishops, in accordance with the recommendations of the Hurd Commission, the workload of Dr Williams will remain excessive. Hence the risk that much of what he has to offer to the Church and the nation, and which requires space for the prayer and reflection he enjoyed as Archbishop of Wales, will be submerged in a ceaseless round of activity.

The demands made on the other bishops are obviously not so great, but they are daunting all the same. In April 2000, the Bishop of St Albans reported that he received more than 10,000 letters every year, besides an even larger number of emails, faxes and telephone calls. He did not say how much of his time was spent attending meetings or travelling to London and what proportion of his ministry was devoted to the pastoral work necessary for maintaining the morale of depressed clergy and failing parishes. The plain truth is that virtually all of the diocesan bishops are trapped in a management system that allows little, if any, opportunity for serious reflection and strategic planning. It is hardly surprising that episcopal ministry restricted to pastoral management has become unattractive to those who are most likely to lead the Church in new missionary directions.

In my book, *The Bishops*[1], I discussed this problem in the context of biographical outlines of the ministries of forty-eight bishops during the period 1830-2000. I concluded that the present bench of bishops is weaker than at any other time during the last 150 years and that this bodes ill for any early renewal of the Church's mission. The book was well received but some of its readers complained that I had been unfair to today's bishops. I welcome the opportunity therefore to affirm my admiration for their pastoral ministries. The Church of England has never been better pastored.

No one asks to be a bishop. An invitation to become one can never be other than a strong vocational challenge. Episcopal ministry is always demanding and, although it doubtless brings its own rewards, the sacrificial element is very considerable. The present bishops are gifted, dedicated and greatly valued by their dioceses. But– and this was the point of my book– their ministries are confined almost exclusively to pastoral management. This is where their skill and experience chiefly lies. They were recruited for this purpose.

Something more is now urgently needed. The Church of England is in an ever-deepening crisis and although 'crisis' is an overworked word it is difficult to find another to describe the present situation. The serious decline in its membership that took place during the second half of the twentieth century now has visible effects in much smaller congregations in most churches, shortage of clergy and acute financial problems. The resources available are too thinly spread to provide a basis for dynamic renewal. All of which, combined with the growth of secularisation, has resulted in the Church being pushed to the margins of society.

This is precisely where the Church stood during the earliest centuries of its existence, yet with the crucial difference that its episcopal leaders were seen as missionary pioneers, rather than as crisis managers. It is this role that now needs to be revived, but this can only happen if there is a bold facing of the facts and a determination to change those aspects of the Church's life that are no longer appropriate to a missionary situation. A business firm facing bankruptcy will fail if its top managers are bogged down with administration and in caring for the anxious staff. New thinking is required.

Much of the present pastoral and administrative work that occupies a diocesan bishop's attention should be reduced in scale and delegated to the suffragan bishops and archdeacons, leaving him or her with time for reflection and strategic planning, based on wide consultation. Such planning will require serious modification of the parochial system and the development of alternative and complementary patterns of ministry, lay and ordained, that will enable the Church to engage creatively with the organs of secular society. This will not bring crowds to fill the empty pews, but is to be seen as a long-term process of challenging and replacing the materialist triviality that stunts so many lives today.

No less important, therefore, is the need to revive the role of the bishop as a teacher of the faith. The present intellectual questionings of the Christian faith are serious and sustained. They cannot be met by hastily composed sermons for confirmation, the institution of new vicars and other parochial occasions. Thoughtful, carefully crafted statements of belief are required and opportunities for serious dialogue with objectors seized. Both of which need space for reflection and prayer.

In short, the bishops need to be liberated for leadership in mission.

**Notes**
[1] SCM Press, 2000.

# Responses

___

### EASTER MORNING

Walking in the garden early, the chill of the cold stone door,
seeing the sun on the pale primroses, aconites and tall narcissi,
glowing gold and lemon in the sparkling dew. Peace filled the air.
After the rending – after the suffering – remembering honest thieves
and thunders raw– I trod in reverie.
I thought I heard a voice and turned to see the gardener–
tending the seedlings, watching the fledglings –
he turned and held my gaze.
'I am not yet ascended,' he said to me. 'Tell them,' he said, 'I am risen'–
words and life of the Spirit to come – 'I am going to my Father –
your Father and my Father – and I will speak more – he is your God
and my God and to recognise it will take many years.'

Patience, I said to the others, patience, my friends.

*Anna Newton*

___

## FROM RICHARD INGRAMS

*Richard Ingrams, ex-editor of* Private Eye, *and now editor of* The Oldie, *regularly plays the organ in Compton and Aldworth parish churches. His most recent books include* Jesus: Authors take sides, *and the authorised biography of Malcom Muggeridge.*

Many of our most venerable institutions– *The Times*, the BBC, the Conservative Party– are currently obsessed with the importance of appealing to the Youth – ignoring, in the BBC's case, such obvious things as the tendency of oldies to stop at home watching TV in greater numbers than young people.

Is the Church falling into the same trap? As a part-time church organist (half-in and half-out) I observe the sometimes desperate measures that priests can go to in their urge to attract a young congregation– the attempts to eradicate anything that might seem archaic, difficult to understand or offensive to modern ways of thought. An obvious example is the editing of the psalms to eliminate those aspects of God that are considered out of keeping with present-day pacifism. In the same spirit the Last Supper in the new Communion service is reduced to Jesus having supper with his friends, 'passover' and 'disciples' being thought to be obscure words.

You ignore at your peril the self-evident truth that religion tends to be something that appeals to men and women as they grow older and get over what Dr Johnson called 'the dissoluteness of pleasure, the inebriation of success, the ardour of expectation and the vehemence of competition'. What is then likely to attract them is precisely the kind of thing so many priests and bishops are seeking to destroy– the old, the challenging, the mysterious.

## FROM DAVID PYTCHES

*David Pytches was Bishop of Chile, Bolivia, Peru; and Vicar of St Andrew's Chorleywood. He is the founder of New Wine Networks, which is impacting the Church of England so profoundly.*

*Here he responds with enthusiasm to the implied vision of our contributors.*
The Church of England will clearly have to make some radical changes to survive the next two or three decades– as I am sure it will. Changes are already beginning to happen. The Diocese of London, the only diocese apparently to have seen real growth over the last few years, is a prime example. In too many other dioceses the hierarchy seem to stare hopelessly into a future of bankruptcy and impotency. In these dioceses, changes have been made more to save money than to save souls. Too many changes appear to have emanated from a management mentality motivated by anything but a creative vision for the future. It may be still too early to assess how productive some of these changes have been but most appear to be grim indeed. At least, however, the Church is getting accustomed to the idea of change and every little we can do to keep the ball rolling (like the circulation of a book such as this) must be welcomed.

> Jesus talked about the problem of putting new wine into old wineskins. The old wineskins resist the fizz of the new wine. They have hardened structures and soon become inflexible. It has been the traditional structures of the Church that have proved to be the most resistant to change, which is exactly what the Lord was talking about. There is nothing wrong with the old wineskins as far as the old wine is concerned. They serve the old wine both fittingly and elegantly. But they serve the new wine poorly. And I would not limit the new wine to what may have become identified with the 'charismatic' movement– though that, too, is certainly a stream from God that should be encouraged and nurtured by the mainline churches. The refreshing life of the Holy Spirit, however, may be discerned in many surprising places. But wherever or whatever the true new wine is, it will usually need the space to flourish and develop its own new structures. In time these can be evaluated and co-ordinated.

> A major problem is that those who are part of an old wineskin often want to dictate exactly what the shape of the new wineskin must be. The challenge today is to allow new wineskins to develop and for those in the old structures to bend over backwards to keep their family links

with them as parents with children– offering help and encouragement when and where it might be called for.

Just one example of the tension between new life and old structures is the problem of traditional parish boundaries. When, some ten years ago, we began to plant out churches from St Andrew's, Chorleywood, I suggested that traditional parochial boundaries had become 'the condom of the Church of England' in so far as they prevented the natural new life that God wants to give us from coming to birth. We needed the flexibility to plant back into other communities, even if they are technically in someone else's parish. Our first efforts at cross-boundary church planting raised howls of protest. It was considered most unprofessional. I have never been totally opposed to the parish concept as there are obviously still some very useful aspects to it, but the idea of 'territoriality' that seems to go with it, needs to be dispensed with.

A book like this, with so much mature reflection, honest insight and far-sighted vision is both stimulating and challenging. Any symposium for a book is usually sniffed at by publishers. But in this book, with its contributions from a fascinating range of churchmen and women, such an approach comes into its own. It offers hope and encouragement to those who believe that there is still time and opportunity to rebuild today's Church

## FROM WANDA NASH

*Wanda Nash (author, most recently, of* Christ, Stress, and Glory*), responds more cautiously than David Pytches. She fears that "the depths" with all its forbidding and potent energy may not have been adequately attended to in this volume. The night is dark as the ocean liner of the Church of England continues to move forward... slowly.*

### New ways of becoming church
When I think of the Church today, I think of a capacious ship ploughing towards uncharted seas at nighttime. It is not foggy, but it is dark. This large,

well-loved vessel, built for families, is still beautiful although her design makes her cumbersome and more appropriate to an earlier way of life. She was built for capacity, comfort and stability; perhaps today we are needing a greater efficiency, more tuned to our contemporary overloaded experience.

In this book we are shown that all around the hull of this ship there are lines of portholes. Each contribution describes one particular porthole, which is lit from within and shines its light into the darkness. Not all of the portholes are the same size or the same shape; not all the available portholes are lit up within these pages, there are gaps between them. Some are giving out a clear beam, some are dimmer and some are half-shuttered. But together they suggest something of the way ahead.

The book offers no single experienced pilot to guide the ship, and by the end of it the darkness is still dark. None of those living within individual cabins could guide the entire ship with their individual lights, but they each add to the visibility of the way. By the end we still can't resolve the unknownness of 'full steam ahead', but that is the nature of our journey.

As I read through the book, there were special beams of light for me which are memorable: I learnt a lot from Tim Dakin's analysis of mission. I personally resonated with the powerful material of Ray Simpson—his phrase 'the spirituality of the shoes' is one I have carried further into my own work.

Nonetheless, there remains a reticence that is common in our Church. We have a reluctance to deal with the plumb physicality of the tools with which God has provided for us to use for the kingdom. Things with which we have been equipped in our bodies, but which are only lent, not given to possess and misuse. We have been given personal responsibility for them, and we are accountable when they have to be returned. And yet the processes of learning how to deal with them is seldom touched upon from our pulpits or, indeed, in our 'religious' literature. We are still rooted in ancient formulations of Augustinian origin: 'Leave it all to God'.

In general, attention to things of the body is seen as a distraction from things to do with the spirit, not as being connected and leading directly to them. It is a strange paradox that the more unearthly and worldly we become, the greater is the temptation to be grounded in concrete. Sometimes, in imagination, in place of stubbornly rock-bound church buildings I have played with wonderful ideas about the use of tents and marquees– colourful, movable, flexible, impermanent. Places become sacred spaces because they are prayed in, not simply because they are hung about with antecedents. I have discovered in war-torn Africa, that holiness clings to an elementary structure prayed in for a few months, quite as much as it does to bricks centuries old. Is it something about the quality of the prayer itself? Trust, play and abandonment are surely primary elements of prayer that signs the future, quite as much as reason, usefulness and obedience. Physically, I look for a place where listening is possible, and receiving from God whatever it is that God wants me to receive, is possible; instead of a place where I am encouraged to keep up a constant bombardment of demands, information, requirements, expectations, projections and endless humanly designed constructs, in the direction of God.

On re-reading that paragraph, I am surprised at the apparent aggression of it! As a child I was brought up in four continents, attending twelve schools. When at home, my mother took me to a different church every week, so I should receive a 'good grounding' in all aspects of Christianity. In adult life, and married to an archdeacon with special national responsibilities, I find I have worshipped in about 250 churches. And everywhere I have found an emphasis on what God can do for me. Like the astonishing honesty of the prisoner who, when asked, 'Why do you come to chapel?', answered without hesitation, 'To see what I can get out of him, in'it?' And I have found thousands of sermons allegedly supplying answers – and this in days when increasingly we know there are no neat answers. Rather than concentrating on 'what can/does God do for me?' isn't it time we spent more prayer on accepting the pure mystery of God? And the non-predictability of God's choices and actions?

For me, it is unknowingness itself that is important. Perhaps the days of being sure about anything are gone; perhaps it is no longer, in our crowded seas, appropriate to proclaim through a megaphone a particular certainty about any direction. Perhaps there are too many different shoals of fish to be attended to by any one ship at any one time. The lights coming from other boats contribute to the light of the whole fleet, whether they are younger or older, whether they are of this shape or that usage.

The one thing each ship has in common is its hull, its hold. This is the strange thing: often it is the nature and contents of the hold that are least open to discussion. Isn't it the ballast in the hold that aligns each ship to its centre? That keeps it upright? It is that which enables it to keep its balance even in the storm.

Much of this book describes the behaviour of players on the bridge, or even, more often, those on the games deck. There is something here about what might happen in the map-room, where the cerebral part of our being works to make a common plan for the journey. Not so much discussion is given to the domestic quarters, where ordinary people eat and sleep, wash and keep themselves socially clean. And those murky spaces where strong emotions are let loose and we make love or make war, where doubt or anxiety are rife, where frustration or hostility, fear or extravagant hope are let out of their cages– the ship of the Church of England is less good at exposing these. If such elemental things are found among those who officiate or in the officiants' families, the Church seldom wants to know. There is not a lot here that leads us to focus on the ballast in the hold, nor about accepting the Unknowingness around about us; is this a reflection of the nature of our Church, or something about the personal reluctance of those who have been trained theologically? The nature of the hold and the reality of unknowingness are both securely rooted in the Gospels themselves.

My personal suggestion about the future of the Church of England is that she should attend to that dark, deep, fluid, wordless place of the ship's hold. It is a place not subject to reason, but it speaks with consistent experience. It is the one thing in common between all the ships sailing in the search for God and godliness, but it resists being canned and tamed and schematised. It not about the power and hierarchy and competition that is evident on the upper decks, but it nurtures compassion and unity and sharing, inclusiveness and commitment. And perhaps– is this true?– it is the one feature of the life of the Spirit that is unalarmed by travelling with Unknowing. Hilary Wakeman has put it this way:

> Christianity can survive – if we are brave. The voices telling us this are getting louder, and in the end maybe the crowd will turn and listen. What will not survive in this new century are authoritarian, hierarchical (and therefore denominational) structures; finance-driven structures; and creeds and doctrines that need re-interpreting line by line before they can be spoken with honesty[1]. What will survive is our experience of God …And one of the deepest ways we know God is through contemplative prayer.

What will survive is our experience of God being incomprehensible, while utterly comprehending each one of us. This is the ballast. By exploring it – both individually and corporately we can let go our need to be humans constantly doing, constantly having, and learn more about humans being, as we were created to be. Adam Smith has said that this is the chief 'means for humanity to bring about the New World Order: Stillness to receive God as God is, and not as what we make of God.'[2]

This stillness is coming into our schools and our prisons; it is being included in drug-abuse rehabilitation programmes, in terminal care, in treatments for alcoholics and secular stress management, to list but a few border-posts I have encountered. Stillness in actual church circles is still considered by the majority to be peripheral; for the Church to survive it must become a central Still Point to which everything else is tethered. As an unknowing child of God, I put myself in the embrace of God whom I cannot know, only knowing that I am totally and intimately known. This is where the exuberant generosity of God and the huge surprise of grace becomes real; and then, hopefully, transferable.

To be practical, for my own part, I have started to distribute what for me is a 'menu' of the future. In my work with clergy and church leaders I have found it speaks strongly concerning how, under God's guidance and in God's embrace, we can begin to allocate the energies with which we are equipped without ultimate risk of burn-out. It is a re-working of the 'spend and be spent' ethic into something more applicable to our overloaded modern circumstances.

The twenty-first century has been acclaimed the 'age of knowledge', and powerful sections of our communities insist that 'knowledge' is the basis of business, of qualifications, management, research and development, and of all sorts of success. Yet in the Church we cannot 'know', with comprehensive certainty, the nature of God, or the why's of suffering, or have any tidy solution to the problems of evil or the outcome of progress. But:

Sometimes, in the place of scientific certainty, we are offered awe and wonder;
sometimes, in the place of activity and busyness, we are offered stillness;
sometimes, in the place of duty and good works, we are offered desire and delight;
sometimes, in the place of solemnity and reverence, we are offered play and laughter;
sometimes, in the place of security and no-risk, we are offered uncertainty and unknowing;
sometimes, in the place of words, beautifully constructed, we are offered wordlessness . . . and silence.

Is the Holy Spirit of God once again turning the tables on us?

---

**Notes**

[1]  Hilary Wakeman, 'Contemplative Prayer and the Future of Christianity' in Hilary Wakeman (ed.), *Circles of Stillness*, DLT, 2002, p.182.

[2]  Adam Smith, 'Meditation—a New Age Phenomenon?, in Hilary Wakeman, op. cit., p. 191.